Every Heart Homeschooling: Joy in Learning

Esther Palmer

ONION RIVER PRESS

Burlington, Vermont

Onion River Press
89 Church Street
Burlington, VT 05401
info@onionriverpress.com
www.onionriverpress.com

ISBN: 978-1-966607-23-6

Library of Congress Control Number: 2025912532

"Will you teach me everything you know?"
the oxherd boy asked.
"I don't think so," replied the ox.
"I'd rather relearn life with you
than simply pass on my old ways."

The Oxherd Boy: Parables of Love,
Compassion and Community
by Regina Linke

When my children were born, I chose to prioritize their wellbeing.

I committed to listening and acting in their best interests.

I respectfully parent—my children are themselves.

Gratitude

I am grateful I took the path less traveled and committed to know and love myself. I am in awe of what I learned and created.

I am grateful to my husband, Tony, for the gifts he has given of time and financial stability.

I am grateful to my best teachers, our three daughters.

My firstborn, Lauren, opened my heart and taught me that to love her is to love myself, that life is joy, and that play is learning.

Aidan taught me to listen and follow and that all is well.

April taught me that I am perfect as I am. *Be still and know.*

I am grateful to Louise Dietzel, my mentor and friend, for loving herself unconditionally. Thank you for shining your light and seeing me clearly when I did not know myself.

Every Heart Homeschooling

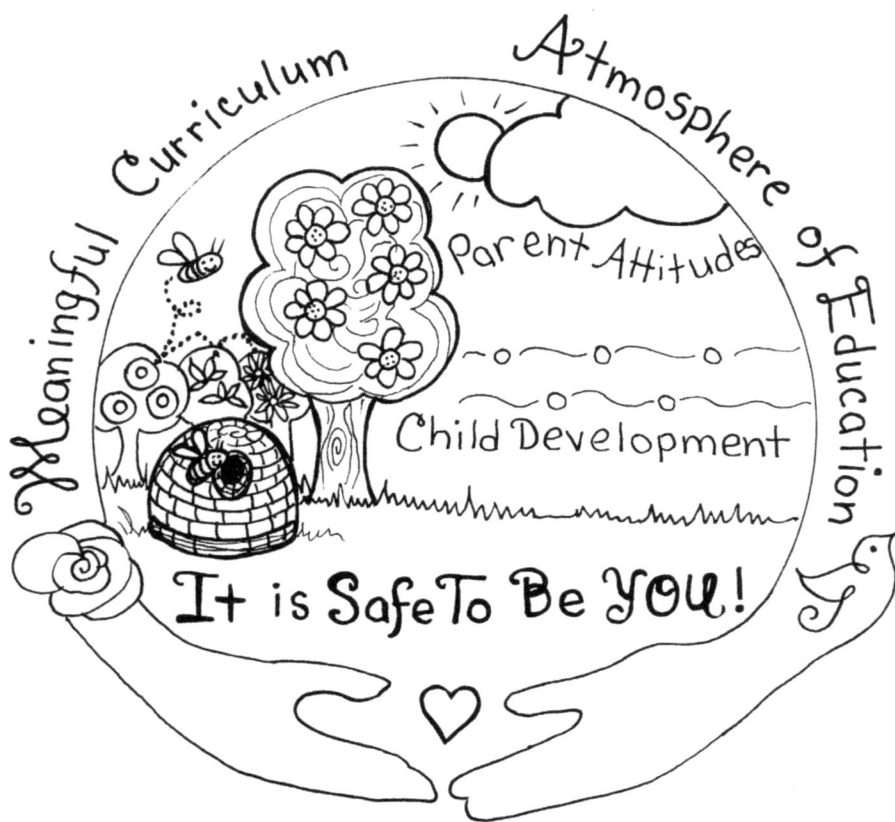

Meaningful Curriculum

Atmosphere of Education

Parent Attitudes

Child Development

It is Safe To Be YOU!

Joy in Learning

Contents

Mission Statement

Joy in Learning
To yourself, always be true.

Mission: To graduate young adults as lifelong learners and critical thinkers who are always curious about themselves and the world.[1]

About: Our education is built on three "Cs": Curiosity, Creativity, and Connections. Project-based learning is prioritized. Students collaborate on course development and guide their own schooling.

---

1   *See Appendix A: School Profile*

Introduction

In the spring of 2022, my husband Tony and I presented a high school diploma to our youngest daughter, April. She was the last child to graduate from our "Joy in Learning" classroom. April chose a close-knit family gathering for her diploma ceremony. A spring cold front necessitated an indoor celebration. We dressed up and settled into the living room for the convocation. Our three daughters' reflections on childhood and education intermixed with pomp and circumstance. Intimate sharing and elegant simplicity made the ceremony extra special.

Our middle daughter, Aidan, chose a backyard commencement under a cascade of willow branches flanked by a cloudless blue sky. We celebrated with family, friends, and mentors, completing the afternoon with traditional fiddle music, singing, games, and picnic fare.

Our eldest daughter, Lauren, received her diploma from public school. After graduation, friends gathered at our home for a celebration in keeping with Bilbo's "eleventy-first birthday party" from *The Lord of the Rings*, Lauren's favorite book. We had games, huge bubble wands in buckets of soapy water, a bonfire, and an abundance of food. The celebration concluded with Scottish bagpipes as the sun set.

For fourteen years I taught Lauren, Aidan, and April, interweaving public school and homeschool. Being their teacher revealed the magic of learner-centered education, preserving my children's sense of self and restoring my own. My approach is novel.

Home education is an immersive, living curriculum that I still cultivate every day. Writing *Every Heart Homeschooling* has reminded me of what I intuitively created. This is a record of my choice, experience, insight, and growth.

Chapter 1

Early Homeschooling: Primary Lessons

My Mentor

I met Louise Dietzel, a psychologist and teacher, at a parenting workshop when Lauren was in preschool. Louise was warm, accepting, and said the most surprising things: "You are amazing! Do you know it?" I did not. I was attracted to this joyful woman who listened attentively and responded in gentle, unexpected ways. She became my mentor and guide. My work restores my awareness of *who I am* as I am the parent I envision. Everyone needs a mentor who knows, values, and loves themselves, and who is then able to see the goodness and perfection in others. A gifted mentor reminds us of *who we are* as we learn to know, value, and love ourselves.

Paying Attention

My childhood taught me to attune to my children. This awareness came from realizing that what I got the most of in childhood, I deserved the least, and what I got the least of in childhood, I deserved the most. I came from a large minister's family where my parents' attention often went to my siblings and community members rather than to monitoring the quality of my schooling. When I became a parent, I pledged to note behavior changes in my children. This was the commitment I made to each child at birth.

In early parenting, I was learning to be a mother to three children while creating a vibrant, healthy home life. Parenting Lauren provided me experience and growth, which in turn modified my approach and responses when parenting Aidan and April. *I continue to alter my choices as I observe, listen, and know. Paying attention comes first.*

My initial awareness that public school may not be a fit for my children came when Lauren began half-day kindergarten. As the year progressed, she came home from school and repeatedly slammed doors—a behavior that was opposite to her bubbly, joyful self.

In retrospect, I realize that Lauren's outbursts at home were an outlet for accumulated frustrations of basic, daily unmet needs: to be seen and recognized as herself. The school curricula, teacher's personality, and classroom environment did not support Lauren's learning style, interests, and uniqueness. I was unaware of this broader perspective at that time, however, and Lauren remained in public school.

First and second grades provided different teachers, different classroom environments, and different curricula. Lauren felt freer and safer to be herself, and the door slamming stopped. Her bubbly self returned.

Lauren's third and fourth grade years were exceptional. She had the same teacher both years. Mrs. Wilson, secure in herself, saw Lauren's strengths and harmonized with her learning style. Lauren immersed herself in big ideas and learned by self-direction. She researched topics of interest, created elaborate presentations, wrote stories, and pursued creative inspirations. In the safety of Mrs. Wilson's classroom, Lauren experienced the heart of true schooling.

Aidan, in public-school kindergarten at that time, was active and happiest when outdoors. The expectations of indoor schooling did not match her need for physical activity. Her level of frustration increased as the school year progressed. The contrast between Aidan's and Lauren's early experiences and Mrs. Wilson's classroom oasis was noteworthy. My curiosity was piqued. How could I gift my daughters joyful education year after year?

The decision to homeschool, not a common decision, took time to become my reality.

Observation Leads to Expanding Possibilities and a New Choice

Awakened to the possibilities of a personalized school experience like I had seen in Mrs.

Wilson's classroom, I determined to explore other educational options. Every alternative that I imagined, however, fell short of meeting my new standard. While sharing this conundrum with a friend, she asked, "Have you considered homeschooling?" I had not. I had biases about homeschooling, which, as most biases do, lacked information. Open to alternatives, I started researching. My relief was immediate—I had options!

We began homeschooling when Lauren entered fifth grade and Aidan entered first grade. Preschooler April joined or played alongside us. We established a classroom, and I purchased a stack of curricula. I quickly discovered that lesson plans guided by subject matter and time restraints are a poor substitute for the natural learning of a child's play-filled days.

The Nature of Learning

My children and I worked in partnership. I was my children's teacher as my children were also my teachers. My confidence in teaching expanded as I began to understand that learning is natural and automatic. Teaching must mirror this "natural education."

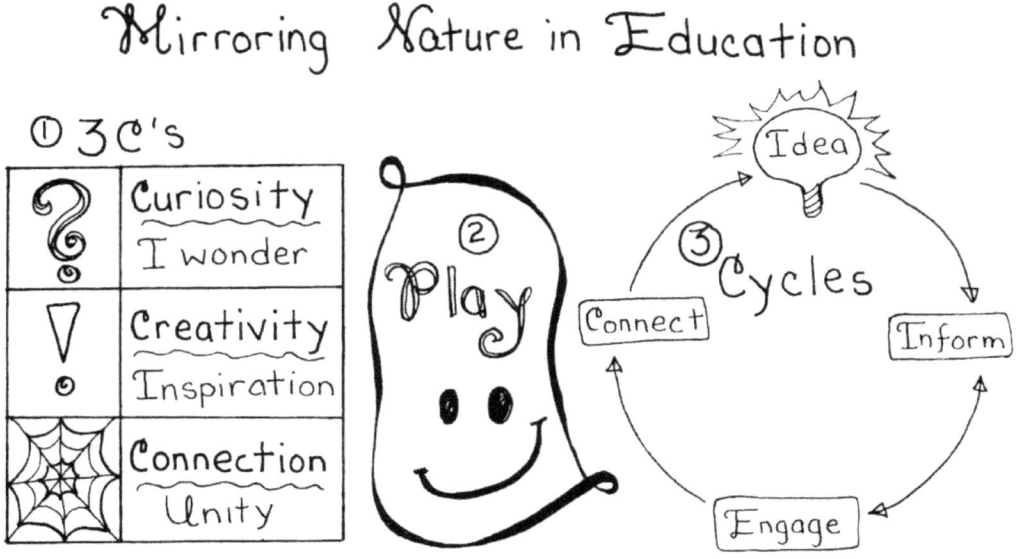

Nature sustains joy-filled learning.

> *In nature we never see anything isolated, but everything in connection with something else which is before it, beside it, under it and over it.*
>
> –Johann Wolfgang von Goethe

There are tandem cycles in natural learning: the *cycle of play* and the *cycle of schooling*. In both cycles, exploring ideas leads to new information. Through experience, personal connections are made and understanding deepens. New ideas arise, and these cycles renew.

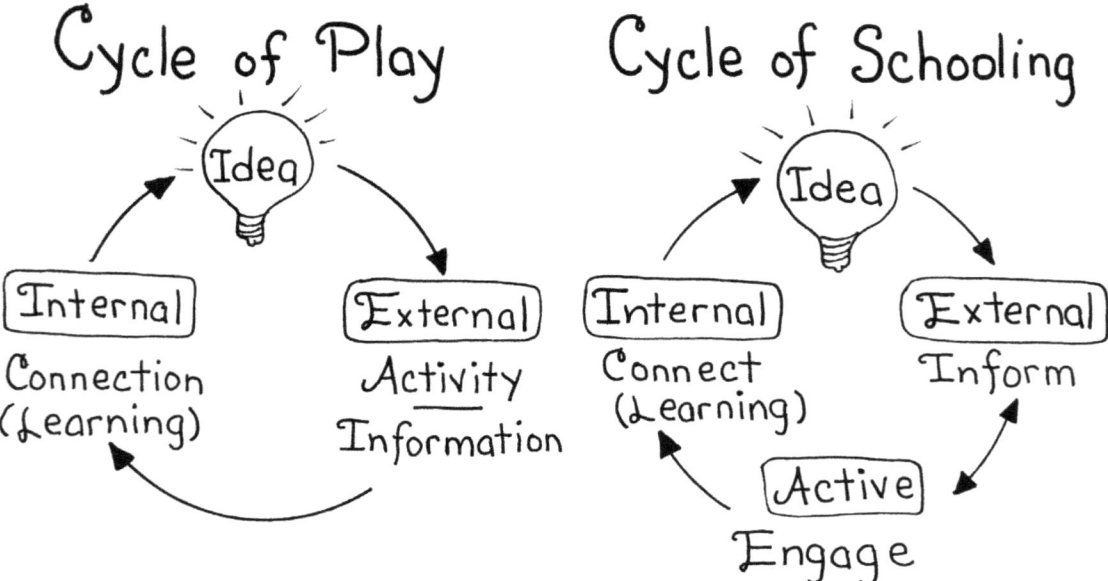

Vivid Imagination Precedes Creation

My girls brought their ideas to life through imagination and available resources. Old clothes and fabric remnants were reconfigured into bandages, doll clothing, and accessories for impromptu plays. Wood scraps found new life as doll crutches, wheelchairs, and all manner of inventions. Couch cushions and bedding became living room forts and homes creatively woven into imaginative play. Cardboard boxes were repurposed as sets for plays or cut, tucked, and glued to create three-dimensional hats and props. Pulleys were engineered between rooms with baskets attached and items conveyed. Health, biology, physics, chemistry, math, literature, writing, arts, problem-solving, and cooperative play wove together seamlessly. Imagination and possibility flourished.

Learning is Play and Play is Learning. I looked for ways to blend instruction with play, dovetailing education with curiosity and creativity.[2]

Poetry Is Child's Play

Our first year, we played with poetry. Lauren, already a writer, enveloped poetry. Aidan, active and artsy, enjoyed poetry embedded in music, movement, and activity. The local library sponsored a community poetry slam. Composing, refining, and practicing guaranteed the girls a place on the local stage. Excitement abounds when education meets imagination and purpose!

We merged poetic picture books and song lyrics with arts and crafts. The girls expressed rhyming, rhythm, and syllables through jumping, skipping, dancing, and hand games. They wrote poems, both structured and free verse. Aidan brainstormed and dictated while I transcribed. Lauren poured over poetry and played with language and voice through verse. At the end of our study, each chose an original poem to illustrate and share at the poetry slam. Aidan draped herself in Lauren's oversized maroon velvet dress and donned earth-streaked sneakers; Lauren wore her cherished horse-clad skirt, vest, and boots—a daily staple. I have sweet pictures of each proudly reading their poems.

---

2   ***See Appendix B: Homeschooling is FUN!***

Aidan

Lauren

Early Homeschooling Revelations

Poetry, music, and movement melded into our daily routine. I added words to an old Shaker tune, "Simple Gifts."

I am whole, I am perfect, I am strong, and powerful;
I am loving, harmonious, and happy.

We created pantomimes for each phrase, magically elevating frequencies as language, movement, melody, and heart unified. *Energy becomes reality.* Love, kindness, and consistency all begin with self-awareness.

While the girls enjoyed this song, it was truly impactful for me. The girls were themselves—effervescent, joy-filled, and open. Through faithful daily practice, *I remembered* who I AM. This song remains my inner mantra today, anchoring my highest choices when challenges come. It is a true reset to inner peace and clarity.

I also memorized these "Rules for Life," which are guides to my well-being:

Rules for Life

I am responsible for myself and to myself.

I create my own experiences and feelings.

When I speak, I say more about myself as what I say about the other person.

At any given time, I am doing the very best that I can do.

I can always be kind and gentle with myself.

—Louise Dietzel, Psychologist-Master

High frequency vibrations create new pathways of thinking, belief, and behavior. As my thinking changed, what I saw and how I responded changed. *Thoughts are energetic.*

Everything is energy and that's all there is to it. Match the frequency of the reality you want, and you cannot help but get that reality. It can be no other way. This is not philosophy. This is physics.

–Albert Einstein

Defining Daily Routine

The girls' creative excitement about classwork and activities often left a mess in the classroom that then spread throughout the house. In the blessed, chaotic atmosphere of our school, it became clear that establishing limits and routines was necessary. I discerned, created, posted, and taught. Once established, my job was consistent maintenance. Defining clear limits and routines within myself and then teaching these to my children led to a relaxed and peaceful classroom and home.

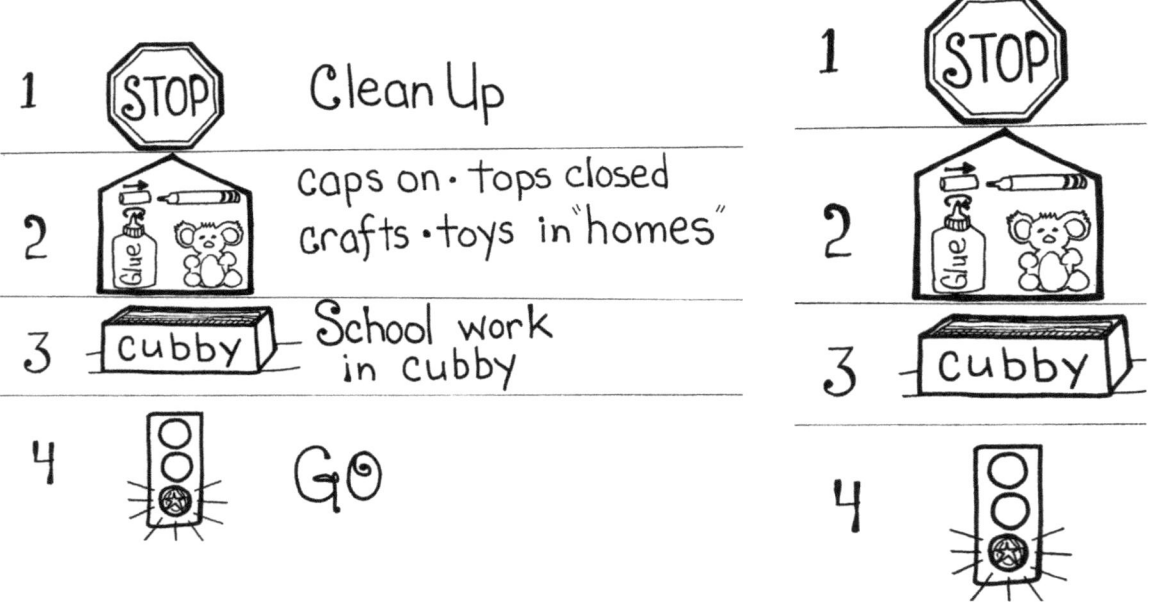

Initially posted Clean Up Routine (left) and later Simple Reminders (right)

Communication and Understanding

Children depend on adults. The extent to which we know and value ourselves enhances our deeper skills of listening and understanding our children.

A child's words and behavior convey a hidden message about their *inner* experience. Like an iceberg, the largest portion of communication is concealed beneath what is obvious.

Discerning a child's MEANING cultivates joyful life and learning.

Active listening **builds trust and safety as we facilitate plans for our child's best growth—it means decoding what our child needs.**

Active listening says, "YOU ARE SAFE TO GROW BEING YOU!"

Chapter 2

Significant Adults Have a Long-lasting Impact

April Begins School

April attended kindergarten in public school, eager to be with her peers. Having learned from Lauren's and Aidan's kindergarten experiences, I took an active role throughout the year. I met with the guidance counselor in charge of kindergarten assignments, ensuring a good class placement. April's teacher, Mrs. Canfield, was warm, dynamic, and attuned to children. She welcomed them, sang with them, and played with them. She communicated with and welcomed parents. April had a great kindergarten year! Even so, she cried at drop-off each day. I concluded that transitions, familiar or new, were stressful for her, and I decided to homeschool the following year. Aidan and Lauren attended public school that year.

Beginning first grade, April was my only student. Little did I know that the following weeks would hold priceless growth for me. There were frequent power struggles between us that had to end. I was teaching April as I had been taught.

In math, I focused on facts, timed tests, rote practice, repetition, and memorization. Predictably, April resisted! Curiosity led me to question: "What is happening *inside* April?" I deduced that fact-recall and timed tests are the opposite of how she processes mathematical concepts and computations. I adapted my teaching to her style of learning. This began our adventures in math: skip-counting through movement and rhythm, ball games, jumping jacks, jump rope, and addition and subtraction using chalked number lines and hopscotch. Movement and fun replaced memorization and pressured recall. Naturally, April's resistance melted away.

I approached reading in the same way as I had initially approached math, teaching as I had been taught. Unlike the creative flexibility I had learned with math, I became more rigid and inflexible with reading. I had no curiosity about April's inner experience and no creative inspirations to alter my approach. I was not listening to April, and she obliged by not listening to me. *No one wins in a power struggle!* Something had to change.

I re-enrolled April in public school for the second half of first grade. After a short observation period, the teacher requested information on April's strengths and current way of processing information. I made an appointment with a learning assessment professional. The gold nugget of that evaluation was knowing that April delves deep into every subject area, exploring all aspects to her satisfaction. This noble processing typically and essentially requires ample time. Unexpectedly, this discovery ignited memories of my own childhood schooling. The pain of judgement and self-rejection, which I had unconsciously carried most of my life, was released in a flood of memories and tears.

Do not train children to learn by force and harshness but direct them to it by what amuses their minds, so that we may be better able to discover with accuracy the peculiar bent of the genius of each.

–Plato

Self-reflection

My own early education included few exceptional teachers who partnered with children as Mrs. Wilson and Mrs. Canfield had. Like many children, I was pliable and eager to please, absorbing and personalizing comments from adults who did not know their influence and importance.

Throughout my life, I have always been a careful reader. I was consistently in the "slow reader" group in elementary school. When offered a speedreading class in middle school, I signed up. Despite my devoted efforts, my pre- and post- semester speedreading tests had identical times and scores. I wanted to learn faster, to recall quicker, to spell better. I judged my character on how my educational aptitude and performance were judged. Sadly, educators at all levels frequently ignore the value and primacy of each individual child, focusing mainly on norms, rules, testing, competition, policies, and budgets. Unfortunately, college classes such as "I am Wonderful, Powerful, and Capable 101" or "Know Thyself 101" do not exist.

I am not alone in this experience. Often, children conform to teaching methods, adults' expectations, and sterile subject matters. A few children defy them. Both groups risk losing a sense of safety in being themselves. Conformity and resistance by their very nature deny innate learning and self-respect.

What I learned about myself in childhood was backward. What I believed was a disability was, on reflection, an extraordinary *ability*. My determination developed academic excellence, patient and thorough reading skills, the capacity for deep understanding, creative problem-solving, and persistence. My learning style and unique gifts are strengths I use to master challenges. I corrected the view I had held about myself from "something is wrong with me" to "it is safe to BE me."

With greater self-awareness and self-correction, I let go of the reading expectations I had unconsciously brought into homeschooling. Simultaneously, reading with my children became a joy. My daughters naturally developed strong reading and comprehension skills in each one's perfect timing. My history taught me to listen to children and to meet them where they are. It also taught me the power that adults have in forming a child's long-term view of themselves.

My experiences are an example of the often overlooked, long-lasting effect adults have on children, and the power of self-correction that is possible as adults become aware.

I've come to the frightening conclusion that I am the decisive element in the classroom. It's my daily mood that makes the weather. As a teacher, I possess a tremendous power to make a child's life miserable or joyous. I can humiliate or humor, hurt or heal. In all situations, it is my response that decides whether a crisis will be escalated or de-escalated and a child humanized or de-humanized.

—Dr. Haim Ginott

Adult Significance

Parents and educators continually impact children in ways they may not recognize. Self-reflection and self-correction are our best tools. Awareness, knowing, and valuing oneself create the tone and atmosphere at home and in the classroom. As adults respect themselves, children do the same. We are our children's mirrors, reflecting self-worth. Our impact is long-lasting.

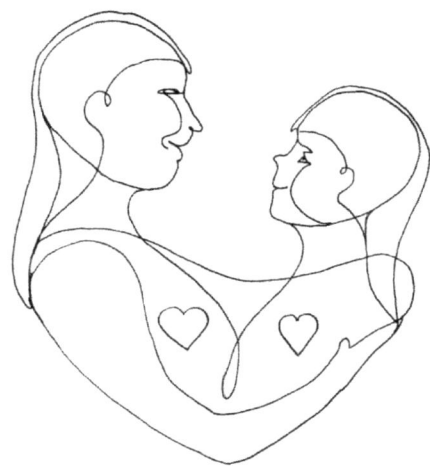

Self-reflection and self-observation illuminate my impact. I ask myself:

Are my words and actions…

…congruent or incongruent?

…kind or hurtful?

…helpful or discouraging?

…trusting or critical?

What is the impact of my words and behavior?

Do I promote inner peace and compassionate understanding?

Do I preserve a sense of goodness and capability?

Do I model self-control and self-esteem?

Recognizing my impact invites personal development.

Self-knowing

We become our best selves as we take responsibility for our thoughts, feelings, and behaviors. When basic needs are met, physical growth happens *naturally* and *predictably*. Emotional growth, however, happens *by choice*. It involves an individual's awareness and contemplation of the existential question, "Who am I?" Our journey of self-knowing, a private and personal process, effects how we relate to our children. *One of the benefits of an adult's self-knowing is always prioritizing a child's well-being.*

Self-Knowing

Close Your Eyes. Fall in Love. Stay There.

–Rumi

Close Your Eyes	Fall in Love	Stay There
I *create* my inner experiences and feelings.	I am doing my best. I can be kind and gentle with myself.	I accept responsibility. I am the adult.
I *focus* on my best choices. Strong emotions invite immature reactivity. I stay out of emotions.	I listen to and follow what I KNOW.	What I say and do is about me. It reflects my *inner* state.
Breathe!	I love and respect myself.	I model maturity for myself. I say what I mean, and I follow through.

Self-knowing is the foundation of life and relationships. *The degree to which we know ourselves is reflected in our attitudes and impact.* A life that is self-known and monitored is happy and productive.

Our thought is the unseen magnet, ever attracting its correspondence in things seen and tangible. Thoughts are electrical and emotions are magnetic. Positive thoughts destroy negativity. Love dissolves anger.

–Louise Dietzel, Psychologist-Master

Chapter 3

Middle Years: Examining Beliefs and Doing What Works

I balanced what was available in our public school with the girls' individual needs and their desire to be with peers. The choice was home school, public school, or a combination of both. If one or all of the girls were in public school, I was central in their education, assuring they were placed in the best classes, communicating with teachers, and supporting them at home.

Middle School

Lauren homeschooled full-time from fifth through ninth grade, with the exception of seventh grade. All three girls attended public school that year: April for the second half of first grade, Aidan for third grade, and Lauren for seventh grade. I was not prepared for the change I saw in middle school culture. The school's attitude shifted from *parents as partners* to *parents as outsiders*. This mindset was striking during Lauren's parent-teacher conference.

Adult and Peer Effect on Lauren

At the fall conference, I initiated a conversation with the Language Arts teacher about Lauren's gifts in creative writing. Totally missing the point of her giftedness, he emphasized that I could see Lauren's journal because she had given him "permission" to share it with me. *People see only what exists in their awareness.*

The interaction was startling. Lauren was twelve years old and entering the complexities of adolescence. The teacher was privileged to see my daughter's assignments and expressions, to celebrate and support her exceptionality—or not—while parents needed permission! The teacher had 80+ students who rotated through his class each week. I had one Lauren. I was attuned to her needs and kept her safe as she grew. *My parent role is primary over anyone in any institution, never to be overtaken.*

Lauren's demeanor and behavior changed throughout that year. Before seventh grade, she was her free spirit, wearing long skirts daily and arranging her hair with copious barrettes or ponytails in various directions. She played with everyone. That year, she was befriended by a group of girls who viewed themselves as popular. They noticed and commented on individual differences. Lauren's clothing and hair styles changed. She spent time grooming in front of a mirror. She was learning to judge and condemn herself.

Lauren was overwhelmed. Her behavior changes signaled a need for my support. I underestimated the impact of this situation, however, and Lauren finished the year at public school.

Parents are the primary influence on children. The environment is secondary. Yet, the setting is important. As we parent, we learn about ourselves in each interaction, always self-reflecting, correcting, and forgiving as we gain experience and grow.

Disturbance—Ponder—Dissect—Change Belief

The blind value I had placed in two unexamined beliefs contributed to the disturbing changes I was seeing in Lauren's behavior. I had accepted the mainstream idea that being with peers is necessary for healthy child development and becoming well-adjusted adults. I had also embraced the adage, "When you start something, you finish it." *Assumptions block active listening.* The discrepancy between beliefs and observed experience cued me to ponder, dissect, and change.

Any environment can affect a child's developing sense of self. The quality and self-respect of people, in any situation, influence children. Adults who live standards of excellence, virtue, consistency, and trust exude the same. The younger the child and the more time spent in any place—whether inviting or hostile, comfortable or disturbing, safe or unsafe—the greater the effect. The stronger a child's sense of self—a process that develops gradually—the less the potential impact of the outside environment. Parents monitor environments, continually assessing what is safe for the child. This is the power of the choice to homeschool. *Safety is a primary parental role.*

With each belief I corrected, each awareness I gained, and each new behavior I practiced, the "good-girl" persona deconstructed itself. *Self-awareness and active responsibility fine-tune what works best.* I pay attention, question, decipher, conclude, and act—all of which are growth-enhancing. The illusion of what appears essential, in time, magically corrects and returns us to our true path.

And now here is my secret, a very simple secret: It is only with the heart that one can see rightly; what is essential is invisible to the eye.

—Antoine de Saint-Exupery, *The Little Prince*

Meeting the Literary Masters

Lauren's eighth and ninth grade homeschool years were magical. She loved to learn and thrived on challenging work, as she still does today. I discovered "Quest," a parent collaborative for middle and high school students. They valued excellence in education and were respectful and inviting. Quest met one day a week with homework assigned for between meetings.

Each parent-educator in Quest was exceptional. Mrs. Crouch, a licensed math teacher, was steady, caring, and clear. She tutored my children for many years. Through her guidance, Lauren, Aidan, and April deeply understood and enjoyed math for the first time.

Mrs. Brennan, Quest's beloved history and literature enthusiast, was also a devoted teacher. Knowing her worth and value, she taught from her heart with curiosity and joy, discovering and celebrating each student. Her enthusiasm was contagious. She made learning fun.

In Mrs. Brennan's classes, Lauren discovered English writer and philologist J.R.R. Tolkien. Early-reader chapter books were left behind, and Lauren eagerly entered the rich world of Tolkien's *The Hobbit* and *The Lord of the Rings*.[3] She learned about medieval England and was inspired at thirteen years old to write a 300-page, Tolkien-style, coming-of-age novel about the courage to be oneself. Mrs. Brennan's enthusiastic commitment to producing Shakespeare plays also sparked a love of Shakespeare in Lauren and other students. *When the student is ready, the teacher will appear!*

Lauren's first Shakespeare production, Much Ado About Nothing, *playing Hero*

---

3   *See Appendix B2: Mystery Feast*

Quest was an exceptional group, where parents and youth shared the delight of living and growing. It is an example of the child-centered education that is possible.

Lauren chose to attend public school for tenth through twelfth grade. Quest students were individuating, their educations diverging. She met graduation requirements through public school while continuing to design homeschool studies to explore her interests.[4]

I Am the Answer

Lauren was in public school when Aidan entered seventh grade and April fifth grade. Their desire to be with their peers continued. I heard about a relatively new private school with twelve middle-school students and one teacher. Parent involvement was welcomed and encouraged. They met in a refurbished barn at the base of Mount Mansfield, Vermont's tallest peak. It appeared ideal. I attended informational meetings, spoke with current students and parents, and met with the teacher. One of the founders was an education professor at a local college. The girls were excited. I signed the contract.

Aidan and April enjoyed their school's nature-centered environment and playing with peers, particularly the boys, who were more inclusive and active than the girls. They were generally happy. I chaperoned monthly field trips and led multiple activities. Each day was full. As the semester progressed, Aidan and April noted a lack of outdoor supervision. The adult responsibilities had insidiously shifted to the students. I spoke with the school chairman and teacher. Little changed.

Christmas vacation, away from school, provided me time to answer the question: "What is happening in what at first appeared to be a perfect learning environment?" Listening to each daughter, coupled with my observations, it was clear that the teacher had personal issues and struggles that were preoccupying her teaching focus. I realized that board members put emphasis on the teaching *role*, missing how the teacher functions *in* the role. They covered up and excused problems rather than addressing and correcting them. When I reflect on the school, on the board members forgetting the school mission statement, on unsupervised students, and on the compromised teacher, it all reminds me of the wisdom

---

4   *See Appendix B1: Living History*

and good judgment I crafted in myself and my daughters.

I requested, and was refused, a refund. I resumed homeschooling, assured that I was the answer to my girls' education. We quickly remediated essential areas of study. *Rebalancing is good!* My takeaway: if it seems too good to be true, examine and examine, as it may be so.

We joined homeschool groups two days a week.[5] Aidan's and April's desire to be with peers was satisfied. The rest of the week was devoted to schooling.[6] I loved being their primary teacher again.

---

5   *See Appendix B5: Community Resources, Woods Group*

6   *See Appendix D: Beehive Study Example*

Chapter 4

Wisdom and Expanding Independence

Through my experience supporting Lauren in high school, I gained confidence. I continued to learn and refine my approach to secondary education with Aidan and April.

Aidan Develops Wisdom

Aidan, following Lauren's lead, planned to attend the public high school. She envisioned exciting and enriched learning opportunities alongside eager peers. When she began ninth grade, she discovered that the truth was the opposite: pressured performance, resistant peers, and teachers who prioritized speed in covering material rather than passion. What she thought it would be, it was not. Within three weeks, she gained new appreciation for the safety, flexibility, and freedom in homeschooling. *Contrasting experience fosters insight, satisfaction, and confidence.*

We resumed homeschooling, and Aidan thrived.

Expanding Independence

Educating adolescents presented opportunities to adjust my teaching approach and to learn more about this important stage of development.

- The main task of *adolescence* is independence and competence.
- The main task of *parenting adolescents* is letting go and trusting.

These tasks take years for child and parent to develop. Remembering your adolescence is a great resource.

In eleventh grade, Aidan took her first college courses: Chemistry 1 and English Composition 1. She took notes, wrote essays, read textbooks, and experienced the rigors of college classes with labs. Such academic demands expanded her executive functions, an example of the Law of Supply and Demand. I helped break Aidan's larger assignments and goals into steps that incorporated time management. I also taught her note-taking and study skills, as well as test-taking strategies, and I encouraged direct communication with professors. Aidan's independence and confidence grew. She learned to monitor her inner state and ask for help when needed.

I continually exercised flexibility and support. When I asked a question one day, I was met with a smile and, "Everything is great!" When I asked the same question the next day, Aidan responded with an overwhelmed and tearful, "Nothing ever works!" Each interaction was another precious opportunity for me to listen and meet Aidan's needs in that moment. *Adolescent fluctuations are wonderful and healthy!*

Wisdom Guides Choices

In young adulthood, discernment grows. For Aidan, college admission requirements, her acceptance letter, communicating with her roommate, and moving into the dormitory yielded soaring hopes that were quickly reversed. Her *picture* of college was not her *experience*. Insight from her ninth-grade public school foray directed her to leave campus within days. My husband Tony and I drove back and brought her home. Realizing that college is not the only option, Aidan soon imagined a new picture of her next steps post high school. She chose a new path, and with her parents' generous support, Aidan is thriving as a potter, remaining true to herself.

April in High School

When April began high school, Lauren had graduated, and Aidan was supplementing her independent high school coursework with college classes. April became my single student, eager for more self-directed education. The awareness and practice of my role in our changing classroom lagged. Our environmental science class was pivotal to my understanding of April's evolving needs and my changing educator responsibilities.

As I had done in previous science classes, I researched the subject, developed interesting activities, and coordinated experiments. However, as the only student, April was not impressed. My determination strengthened. My partnership with April was missing our *collaboration*. She had no interest in a subject she did not know and a class she had little input in developing.

Striving to tailor my approach to this new dynamic, I sometimes inadvertently personalized April's disinterest and reacted. "You have no idea how much work I put into making this interesting for you!" My reactivity invited resistance, and April obliged. Owning my part in these interactions reminded me of several important lessons:

- Kids will not understand or appreciate my efforts—they are kids! It is *my* job to recognize myself *and* them. I am the adult.
- Accept. Let go of expectations. Do not personalize. This is *April's* experience.
- *Understand adolescent stages and tasks.*
- Actively listen for *meaning*.

My approach softened. I created an overview for each unit, and then April guided further study. She researched curiosities, created projects, and shared information. Her interest in environmental science grew. The class culminated in a library display that highlighted environmental issues in our town, state, and country.[7]

Children grow. Educators catch up, adjusting our responsibilities, while increasingly letting go and trusting.

---

7   *See Appendix B6: Library Displays.*

Environmental Science: April collecting water samples from local wetlands

Subjects Connect Through Independent Study

Subjects merge through inquisitive exploration. In April's ninth grade environmental science class, self-directed research into the source of plastics led her to discover the 2010 Deepwater Horizon oil rig explosion in the Gulf of Mexico. The damage was widespread, including along the fragile coast. The following year, April's tenth grade geometry class revealed unexpected connections to environmental science. In the final month of geometry, devoted to real-world application, April discovered Benoit Mandelbrot's book, *The Fractal Geometry of Nature*.[8] Fractals are repeating patterns mirrored in the microscopic and macroscopic world. Fractals underly the order in a pinecone, a head of broccoli, and the circulatory system. Coastlines, too, are complex fractals. This discovery merged two diverse subjects in April's education. Independent study reveals that no single subject is isolated in nature. These connections deepen learning and broaden understanding.

---

8   *See Appendix B1: Field Experiences*

Chapter 5

Homegrown Curricula and Recordkeeping

> *If you have built castles in the air, your work need not be lost; that is where they should be. Now put the foundations under them.*
>
> —Henry David Thoreau

State Law Compliance Becomes a Helpful Structure

Vermont has changed homeschooling requirements in the last few years. When we homeschooled, Vermont law required families to file a yearly Minimum Course of Study (MCOS) for each child. The MCOS, created by the parent, states *minimum* subject goals for the school year. I assured these were met and loved the freedom to teach and expand beyond our stated goals. I reviewed each child's MCOS through the year, modifying and refocusing our studies as necessary. Building yearly education on MCOSs also ensured continuity year to year.

An MCOS includes:

- Reading and writing: communication
- Mathematics: numbers, shapes, conceptual and real-world use
- History: history, citizenship, government
- Literature: fiction, non-fiction, poetry, plays, original source material, research books
- Science: Earth science, biology, chemistry, physics, astronomy
- Movement and health: self-care
- Creative arts: music, fine arts, theatre arts, and practical arts such as sewing, needlework, woodworking, cooking, pottery, menu planning, or architecture[9]

The State of Vermont also previously required proof-of-learning at the end of each school year. Our creative and orderly recordkeeping throughout the year made this easy. Lauren, Aidan, and April filled large tote bags with lapbooks, subject journals, photographs of events, and artwork before meeting with a licensed teacher. With ample time for each child to share memorable learning and highlight their accomplishments, this was a yearly rite-of-passage the girls excitedly anticipated.[10]

---

9   *See Appendix C: April's Fifth Grade Minimum Course of Study (MCOS)*

10   *See Appendix B4: Creative Recordkeeping*

Translating MCOS Plans into Daily Education

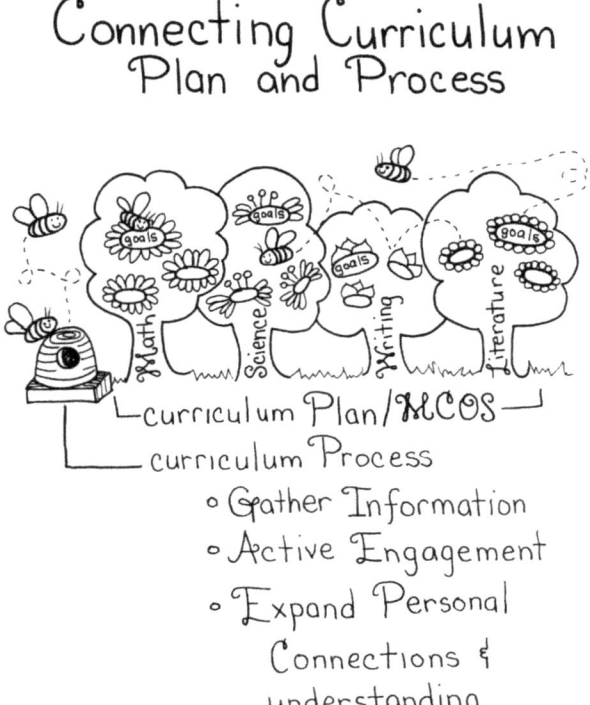

A meaningful curriculum connects goals with interests and is individualized for the child.

- Great ideas and exciting curricula on paper may or may not translate into vibrant learning. Adjust accordingly.
- Assure that activities, interests, and studies are motivating and exciting.
- Let go of expectations. Honor each child's pacing.
- Incorporate Field Experiences. These experiences actualize academic learning. They are satisfying, exciting, and vitalizing, renewing energy for formal study. In middle and high school, purchased curricula, especially in math or science, is increasingly technical. Often concepts and skills are isolated from a child's lived experience. Taking breaks from curricula

allows students to personalize learning. They can research associated questions, create projects, explore interests, and devise experiments.[11]

Beehive Studies

Understanding how goals and activities connect helped me create curricula, modify purchased curricula, and support life learning. The following steps highlight my approach, which I call "Beehive Studies."

Step 1. Curriculum Plans (Goals): Create an MCOS for each child.

Step 2. Knowing Your Children: Be open to the myriad possibilities for meeting goals through engaging activities. This attitude builds bridges.

Step 3. Project Outline: The bridge between *plans* and *process*.

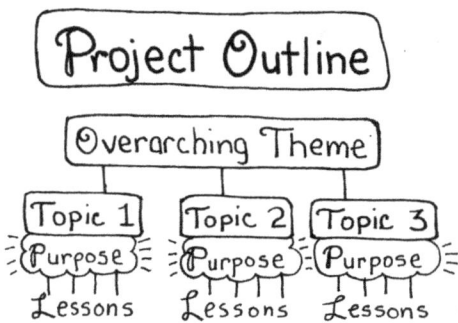

---

11 *See Appendix B1: Field Experiences*

Themes also develop in myriad ways. Examples include wolves (a child interest), *To Kill A Mockingbird* by Harper Lee (a book), snowstorm (an opportunity), poetry (an MCOS goal). A theme often incorporates multiple *topics*.

The *purpose* of an overarching theme or a topic is to engage *imagination*. A child's imagination is their magic, purpose, learning, and play.

Lessons introduce and guide exploration.

Project outlines can be detailed, loosely defined, or spontaneous.

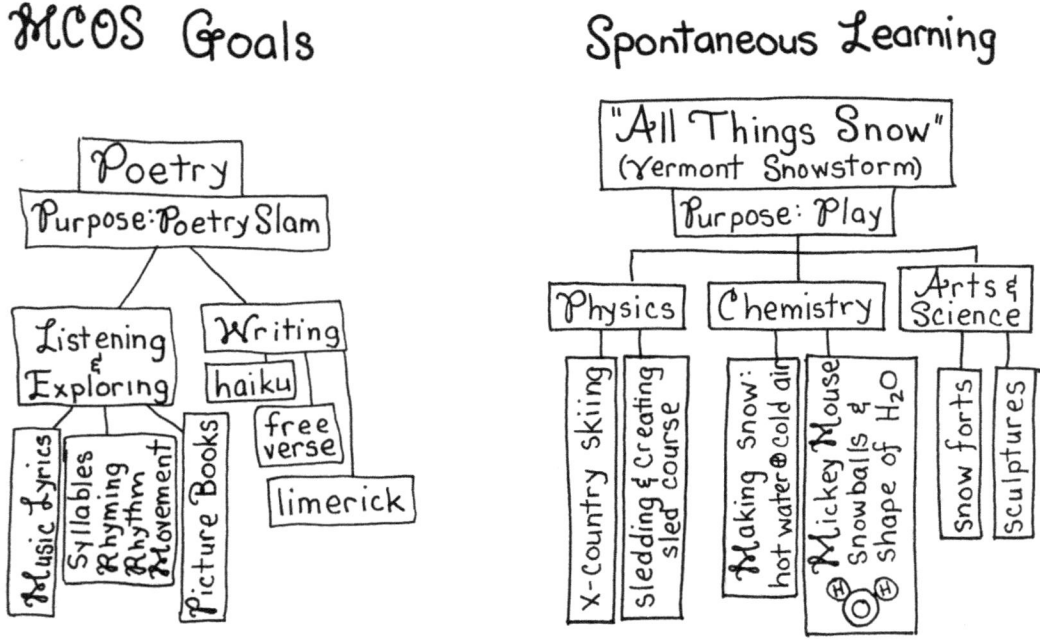

Two diverse examples of project outlines. The poetry unit was detailed in Chapter 1.

Step 4. Cycles of Learning: Cycles flow between your *project outline* lesson plans and a child's expanding ideas and questions. These *start points* direct information and engagement. Cycles of learning are observed in play and mirrored in school.

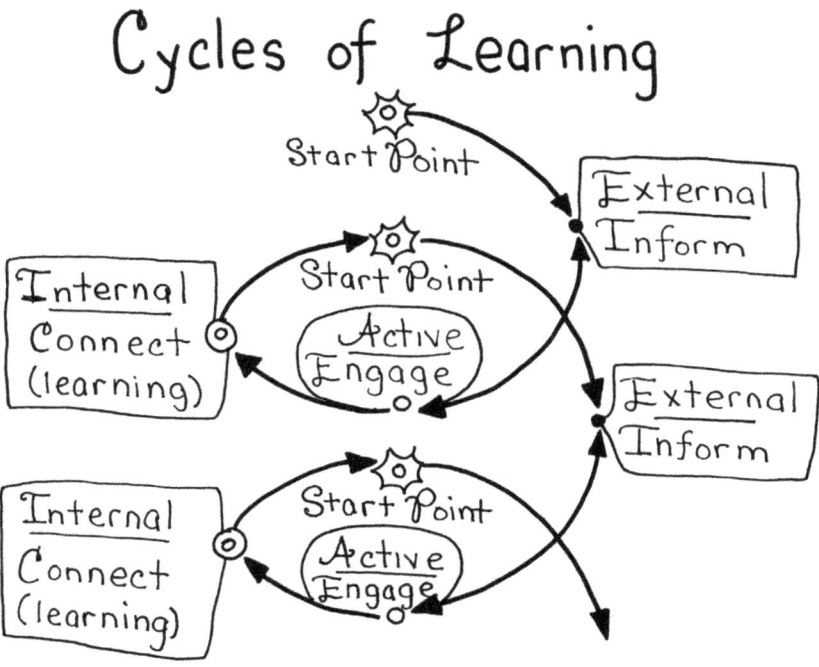

Cycles of Learning

Start points are teacher-guided lessons or student-guided questions.

Step 5: Reflection is essential for an adult's growth. It is a primary tool that teachers use to discern what worked well, what did not, and what to change going forward.

Children are not miniature adults! Reflection is a skill your child will develop in their own timing. Observe your child's curiosity, spontaneity, and excitement. When a big idea or project does not work as planned, give them the gifts of your understanding and connection. Reflection develops in safety.

One of our favorite Beehive Studies explored the 1930s.[12]

---

12 ***See Appendix D: Beehive Study Example***

Curriculum Planning

In elementary school and early middle school, my children shared ideas and interests that I developed into Beehive Studies. As they got older, they increasingly developed and led studies independently. Some of their favorite self-designed high school courses included:

- Playing with Shakespeare: introducing young children to Shakespeare through storytelling inspired by *A Midsummer Night's Dream*
- Puppetry: making fully jointed, life-like animal puppets incorporating biology, physics, engineering, and artistry
- How Things Work: mechanics in the real world
- Kiri-e: traditional Japanese papercutting

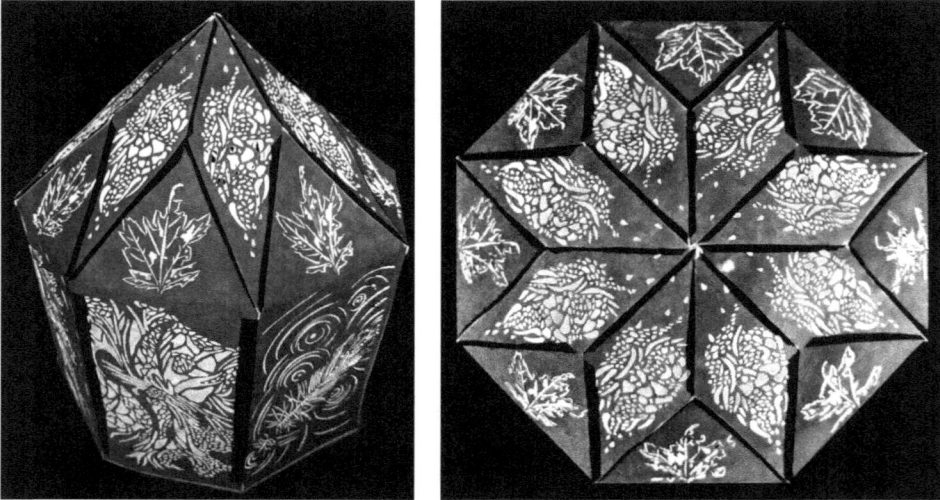

April's Kiri-e lantern: self-designed, inspired by the seasons

- Transcendentalism: Thoreau and Emerson past and present
- Experimentation versus the Known: *Peer Gynt* by Henrik Ibsen and *Frankenstein* by Mary Shelley

High School Administrative Responsibilities[13]

<u>Transcript</u>: Conveying independent learning and Beehive Studies in an official transcript blends information with creativity.

When April was in ninth grade, Lauren, having graduated, taught a year-long class connecting literature, writing, and history. April was the single student. Class met three mornings a week with additional reading, writing, and project-based homework. On April's transcript, this comprehensive class was recorded as three courses. A fourth course emerged from April's research into women's traditional hand crafts of the 1800s.[14]

English	Young Perspectives: Literature	1 credit	A+ 4.0
English	Young Perspectives: Writing— Creative and Technical Writing for Self-expression	0.5 credit	A+ 4.0
Social Studies	Historical Panorama of Cultures Through Time	1 credit	A 4.0
Practical Arts	Fabric Arts: Elements of Design, Technique, Application	0.5 credit	A 4.0

---

13 *See Appendix G: Recommended Resources, High School Recordkeeping*

14 *See Appendix E: April's Official Transcript*

<u>Course Descriptions</u>: Each transcript entry has a corresponding course description. These include grading criteria and credits, which I have omitted here. Course descriptions for the above transcript selections are as follow:

English—Young Perspectives
- **Literature**: Year. April read and discussed four books: *Sense and Sensibility* by Jane Austen (Regency Period); *Great Expectations* by Charles Dickens (Industrial Revolution/Victorian Era); *Little Women* by Louisa May Alcott (Civil War Era); *Testament of Youth* by Vera Brittain (WWI).

English—Young Perspectives
- **Writing—Creative and Technical Writing for Self-expression**: Semester. Concurrent with Young Perspectives—Literature. Coursework included: journaling, creative writing, poetry, compare/contrast essays, a persuasive essay, and a research paper.

Historical Panorama of Cultures Through Time: Year. This survey course covered seven historical periods: Ancient Rome, the Vikings, the Regency Era, the Industrial Revolution, the Civil War, WWI, and WWII. Focus: general history, technological changes, and social impacts. Each unit culminated in a final project. This class provided historical context for *English—Young Perspectives*.

Fabric Arts—Elements of Design, Technique, Application: Semester. In this self-designed course, April explored hand crafts of the 1800s: embroidery techniques, whitework, beading, three-dimensional fabric embellishments, and clothing design and construction.[15]

---

15 *See Appendix F: Course Descriptions*

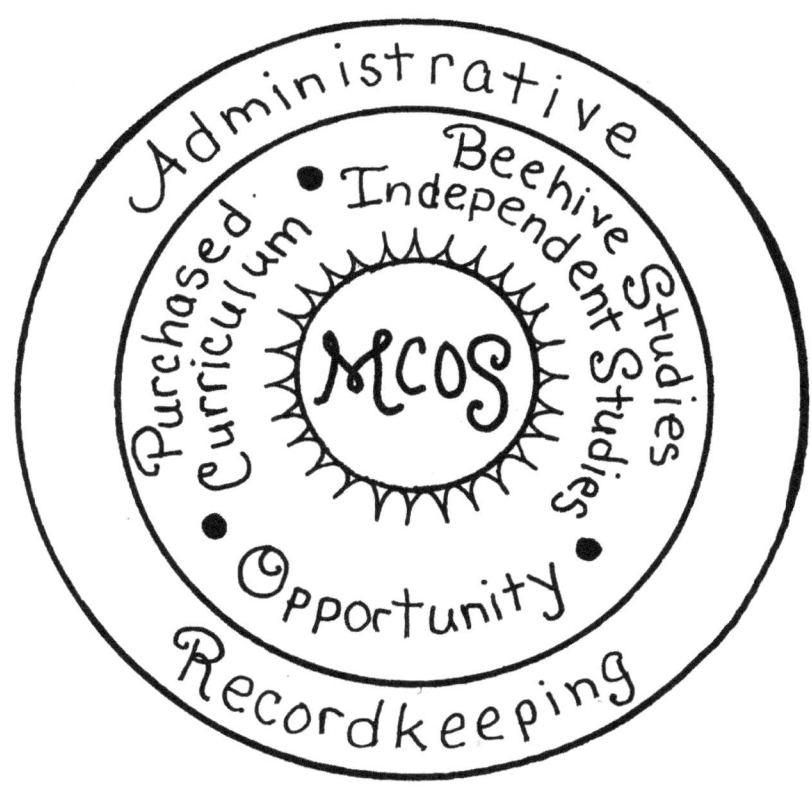

Homegrown Curriculum and Administrative Responsibilities

1 Curriculum Plans: MCOS

2 Curriculum Process: Day-to-day Learning

3 Administrative Recordkeeping

Graduate April with Lauren (left) and Aidan (right)

Chapter 6

Priceless Outcome: Three Happy Young Adults

Today, Lauren is a visionary educator, writer, translator, poet, and storyteller. She remains active in the homeschooling community. Her unbound imagination, curiosity, and playfulness steer her eclectic interests and diverse learning. She is a licensed K-12 Latin teacher.

Aidan is a potter, athlete, and naturalist. She unifies nature, arts, and sciences in hand-crafted clay and glazes, intricately carved and cut vases, whimsical mugs, and elegant teapots. Her pottery conveys the joy and beauty of her life.

April is a gifted artist, a hand-drawn animator, and an administrative assistant. Her attention to detail, patience, and insight yield timeless storytelling masterpieces. Her genius manifests in oil painting, illustrations, and movie-making splendor.

Each is secure and sustained through their own gifts and talents, education, experiences, and skills. I took the road less traveled, and I am blessed. The gift of homeschooling was a priceless investment in my three daughters' lives. All is well!

Every Heart Homeschooling

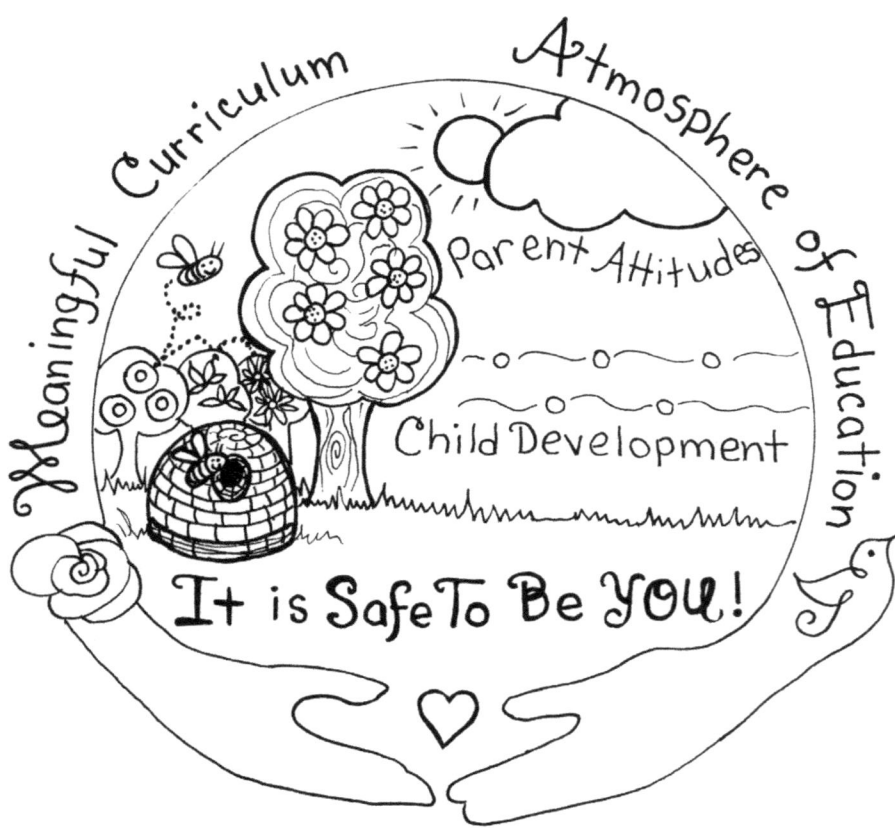

Joy in Learning

Little by little, the sparrow grew
stronger. "We'll take care of
him until he's ready to fly," said the oxherd boy.

The rabbit began to worry.
"But then he might leave us."

"Isn't that the point?"

***

"It's nice the cage will always keep
me from falling," the sparrow said.

The oxherd boy shook his head.
"You're not safe because of the cage,
but because you have wings."

The Oxherd Boy: Parables of Love,
Compassion and Community
by Regina Linke

Appendix A: School Profile

This document consolidates a school mission statement and graduation information for prospective colleges.[16]

Joy in Learning
To yourself, always be true.

Mission: To graduate young adults as lifelong learners and critical thinkers who are always curious about themselves and the world.

About: Located in Vermont's Champlain Valley, our education is built on three "Cs": Curiosity, Creativity, Connections. Project-based learning is prioritized. Students collaborate on course development and guide their own schooling.

Curriculum: We follow the State of Vermont public high school requirements for graduation.

---

16   *See Appendix H: Recommended Resources, High School Recordkeeping*

Students must complete a minimum of 20 credits, which include:

English/Language Arts: 4 credits

Social Studies: 3 credits, including 0.5 credit of U.S. History and Government

Mathematics: 3 credits

Science: 3 credits

Practical Arts: 0.5 credit

Fine Arts: 0.5 credit

Physical Education and Health: 1.5 credits

Electives: 3.5 credits

Additional Schooling Institutions:

Champlain Valley Union High School

Individual classes

Dual enrollment and early college through the Vermont Department of Education

Community College of Vermont

Smithsonian Institute and George Mason University, Early College Program

Appendix B: Homeschooling Is FUN!

I am all for teachers who can make their subjects interesting, who can make them live.

–A.S. Neill

Contents

NOTE: Activities can be adapted for most grade levels. *Examples are grade specific as noted.*

B1. Embedding Education in Play

Field Experiences: Taking breaks from a structured curriculum provides opportunities for students to explore associated questions, interests, and real-world connections.

- *Middle/Early High School*—Students in our Earth science class hosted the annual homeschoolers' Cardboard Box Regatta one year. Each participating family brought duct tape, cutters, and large cardboard boxes. Children formed groups, then designed and built boats. Earth science students assisted children, organized boat launch activities, and created participation awards. During this activity, Earth science, physics, math, engineering, arts, and leadership merged.

Cardboard Box Regatta

- *High School*—During the last month of chemistry, April studied the chemistry of cooking. She read the book *Salt, Fat, Acid, Heat,* by Samin Nosrat and watched Alton Brown food chemistry videos. We were treated to delicious meals, desserts, and drinks, accompanied by April's explanations of the chemistry in each dish.

Living History: Living history connects information, imagination, and activity.

- *Elementary/Middle School*—History, Arts, and Sciences: Studying ancient history introduced us to cave art. Inspired, we taped brown paper to a basement wall to simulate a rocky cave. The girls collected dirt, rocks to crush, and a variety of weedy "brushes." They conducted experiments to determine each rock's relative hardness. These experiments spurred hours of additional rock collecting and pounding. We made paint using dirt, rock dust, acrylic paint, and water. Experience and observation inspired the girls' paintings.

Aidan's cave painting

- *Elementary/Middle School*—History and Dress-up: While studying Ancient Greece, the girls drew Doric, Ionic, and Corinthian columns and taped them to our family room wall. Lauren and Aidan dressed April as Athena, the goddess of wisdom, completing the transformation of our living space into a Greek temple.

April as Athena, goddess of wisdom

- *Middle/High School*—History, Arts, and Journalism: While studying the Age of Exploration, Aidan and April also learned about journalism. They each created a period newspaper to print and share.

- *Middle/High School*—History Reenactment: In twelfth grade, Lauren taught a six-week Revolutionary War class for middle schoolers. The once-a-week study ended with an overnight Revolutionary War "encampment" at our home. Lauren designed a live-action event and assigned roles for her students. These roles included two secret spies with missions (participants were tasked with discovering the spies), camp jobs, interactions with "locals," and missions to complete within the military ranks. We made supper and breakfast over an open fire and welcomed a Revolutionary War reenactor. The spies completed their missions— their identities remained undiscovered!

B2. Embedding Education in Play: Mystery Feasts

The Quest homeschool cooperative introduced us to Mystery Feasts. These events became the favorite of favorites. Parents plan and make food in secret and then create a coded menu for students to order from. The goal of a Mystery Feast is for participants to decode menu items throughout the dinner. The feast IS the mystery.

Theme: A Mystery Feast is themed. It can be based on a time period, historical event, book, or another theme. Participants come in costume.

Coded Menu: Parents create two separate menus for a Mystery Feast: a menu key for parents to serve from and a coded menu for students to order from. Menu items include the food, a napkin, utensils, and drinks. The menu has clues embedded in each item's coded name, connecting the item to the theme and matching the character of the item itself. For example, eggrolls are listed as "Out of the Frying Pan" on *The Hobbit* themed coded menu (page 54).

Ordering: Parents determine how many courses will be served and how many items will be ordered per course. For example, we typically had twelve menu items per Mystery Feast: four courses with three items ordered in each. Students order each course at the same time, independently choosing their coded items. Parents are waiters and fill orders using the menu key. Students must finish ordering the entire menu before seconds of any item are served. It can take many rounds of ordering for students to begin to identify which dishes or utensils match which coded items on the menu. Tip: Keep the portions small.

The Fun of Breaking Rules: Students only receive what they order. Remember that coded menu items include food, all silverware, drinks, and a napkin. Depending on their order, participants may need to eat with their hands, sometimes with a butter knife, occasionally with a fork or spoon. Sometimes they receive a drink, napkin, and fork but no food and watch everyone eat before they can order another course. Sometimes, dessert comes before dinner. Kids love permission to break social etiquette, and they enjoy solving a good mystery!

<u>Additional Activities</u>: Associated activities enrich the atmosphere and experience of a Mystery Feast.

Example: *Middle/High School—The Hobbit* by J.R.R. Tolkien
In eleventh grade, Lauren designed and taught a history and literature class for middle schoolers. Students read *The Hobbit* and learned about English medieval history. The final class activity was a Mystery Feast.

Students received the following invitation:

The Hobbit Mystery Feast coded menu and menu key:

CODED Menu (Students)	KEY (Parents)
What's in My Pocketses?	Bao buns (tofu or meat wrapped in small breads or lettuce leaves)
Out of the Fying Pan	Eggrolls
Barrels Out of Bond	New potatoes with gravy and a sprinkle of parsley
Mirkwood	Broccoli
Desolation of Smaug	Blended squash or sweet potato soup topped with chopped red pepper (pinch of cayenne?)
Trolls' Hoard	Many-layered casserole (lasagna)
The Battle of the Five Armies	Five-veggie Salad
Arkenstone	Mini cupcakes with frosting and fresh blueberries
Spider's Legs	Fork
Bard's Arrow	Butter knife
Thorin's Key	Spoon
Bilbo's One Wish	Napkin
Beorn's Bees	Ginger lemonade with honey

Note: For a Mystery Feast the menu items (food, utensils, drinks, etc.) would be intermixed so that *placement* within the coded menu *is not a clue*. In this example, I have not done this. I have grouped items by category to aid understanding.

The Hobbit Mystery Feast additional activities: Students solved a Tolkien-style Elvish riddle as the password to enter the candlelit medieval "dining hall." At the feast, each participant received a coded menu to order from and a pen to record their guesses. Our Mystery Feasts concluded with associated games and outdoor fun.

The Hobbit *Mystery Feast participants*

B3. Books, Books, Books!

We love bookstores, especially used bookstores and local book sales. Many of our Beehive Studies started as, or incorporated, book sale finds.

- *Elementary/Middle School*—One school year, our geographic exploration revolved around the book *Sundays at Moosewood Restaurant* by The Moosewood Collective. Recipes in this book are organized by world cuisine. Each month, the girls chose a geographic region from the cookbook to explore through recipes and research. Geography, culture, and cuisine melded as we cooked our way through the book.

- *High School*—At a local book sale, April found *Total Peace* by Ely Culbertson, published in 1943. During a self-designed "History in Film" class, she incorporated passages from *Total Peace* that highlighted the role of propaganda in conflict, the necessity of critical thinking, and the courage to be true to oneself.

B4. Creative Recordkeeping

Personalized recordkeeping is engaging and fun to review, strengthening memory, fostering new connections over time, and creating a record of development.

Lapbooks: *Elementary/Middle School*—Manila-folder lapbooks are well-suited for a theme with multiple topics. They blend cognitive expansion with creative expression. Each lapbook reflects its maker. Lauren created elaborate fold-out pages and miniature booklets glued in place or tucked into pockets. Her finished lapbooks were library-worthy resources. Aidan incorporated mechanics and experimented with revealing what she learned through pop-up and interactive elements. April, the designer, crafted highly ordered, neat lapbooks, embellished with craft materials or thoughtfully patterned by hand.

Lauren's ancient history lapbook. The pages were expanded by creating fold-out flaps, adding envelopes for material, etc.

Aidan's pop-up jack rabbit accents information about the Dust Bowl.

Bookmaking: A personally crafted book makes every subject special.

<u>Origami Books</u>: *Elementary*—For Aidan, handmade books elevated challenging writing activities to works of art and exciting projects. Aidan's "All About Me" book has eight pages, each with a fact about herself and an illustration. The pages are folded and glued, and covers are added. A string and button keep the book closed, making it a pocket-sized 3" x 3" when folded.

Aidan with her origami book "All About Me"

B5. Community Resources

National Parks Service Traveling Trunks: The National Parks Service has many "Traveling Trunks" with specialized curricula. Teachers can rent these trunks for a specified time. Study materials are grade-range specific and unique to that National Park. For example, the Ellis Island National Park Service's "Park in a Pack" is geared toward 4th–8th graders and details the history of Ellis Island, immigration, and the Statue of Liberty. Search "The National Parks Service Traveling Trunks" online to discover many options. Tip: Trunks are not centrally located. Check search results for various parks.

- *Elementary/Early Middle School*—We rented a "Wolves Traveling Trunk" from Voyageurs National Park in Minnesota. It included animal track molds for making plaster casts, hands-on resources, multiple books and curriculum ideas, and the skulls and teeth of Ungulates and Canidae.

Aidan's science fair project using the "Wolves Traveling Trunk"

Colleges:

Science Labs and Specialized Information: One of our local colleges, St. Michael's College, includes community outreach in its mission statement. I worked with multiple heads of departments to coordinate upper-level science labs for teens.

- *Middle/High School*—Some examples of our on-campus labs included: a physics lab on light waves, color, and stars; a biology lab on mitosis and meiosis; and a geology lab viewing rocks and minerals through microscopes.

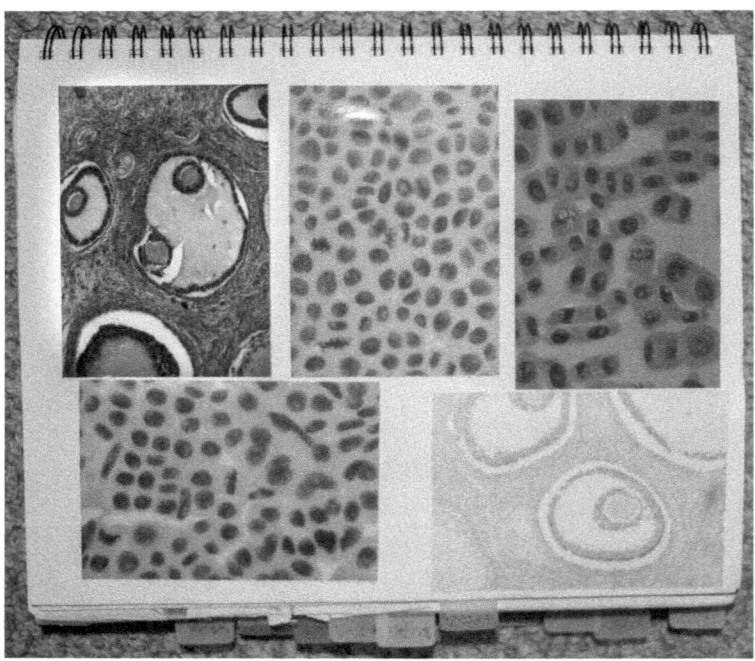

Microscope pictures from the mitosis and meiosis lab at St. Michaels' College

<u>Hiring a College Student</u>: *Middle/High School*—As my daughters became interested in higher-level academics, I sought tutors through St. Michael's College. We hired a writing mentor for Lauren as she edited her novel. We also hired a Latin tutor for April.

<u>Extension Offices</u>: *Elementary/Middle School*—The University of Vermont Extension Office provided us with fertile eggs, incubation equipment, and lessons on embryology. We returned the chicks after they hatched, and they were placed with local farmers.

Lauren with a newly hatched chick

Local Resources and Community Members:

- *All grades*—Members of our local historical society shared stories and artifacts about Vermont in the early 1900s.

- *All grades*—For a homeschool community event, I coordinated a "Tour of the Night Sky" with the local astronomy club.

- *Older Elementary/Middle School*—While studying the Revolutionary War, we read *Champlain and the Silent One* by local author Kate Messner. This book study expanded to a "Meet the Author" homeschooler's event.

Local author Kate Messner presenting on her book, **Champlain and the Silent One**

- *All grades*—We met with six families for a once-a-week, year-long "Woods Group" at a nature park. Morning routines each week included setting up a large shelter, quiet observation and journaling time, and a parent-led lesson with associated activities. Afternoons provided time for student-directed games and unstructured play with friends. Parents shared leadership responsibilities.

Students pair up for a Woods Group activity.

B6. Library

Display Cases: *These require 4–6 weeks of focused research and creation.*

For year-long classes, I often contacted our local library early in the school year to book their large display case for the second semester. As the school year progressed, students worked independently, or in groups, to create shelf displays.

<u>Foundations to Build On</u>: The first few months of any class establishes a routine and a base of information. With this foundation, students can expand upon interests as they develop their displays.

<u>Parent Involvement for Student Success</u>: Coordinating displays for a floor-to-ceiling library display case is a huge project that requires parental support. It also requires devoted in-class and out-of-class time. Generally, the younger the student, the more structure, guidance, and support they need.

<u>Choosing a Theme, Researching, and Building the Display</u>: Approximately six weeks before our library display, I devoted regular class time for design. I facilitated brainstorming with clear project parameters and focused directions. As a group, students reflected on what they had learned in class, chose an overarching theme, and defined individual topics for shelf displays. Depending on their level of independence, students can research and create shelf displays at home or in class. An educator's clear structure, regular check-ins, and incremental due dates ensure success.

Examples:

- *High School*—Environmental Science: April and I created this display together. Topics included local hiking trails and unique ecosystems, stormwater runoff management, water quality testing, petroleum products, and the Deepwater Horizon explosion.

Environmental science display bottom shelf: local trails, habitats, and unique ecosystems

- *Middle School*—Earth Science: Four students created this display. Topics included tectonic plates, volcanoes, layers of the earth, fossils and geologic time, the water cycle, and erosion. Students also crafted a pictorial geologic time scale for the children's library.

- *High School*—Africa: One student detailed layers and ecosystems of the African rainforest for the backdrop. Four students created shelf displays. Topics included arts, geography, culture, animals, prominent individuals and organizations, and refugees.

Middle and top shelf of our World Geography and Arts class display about Africa.

Art Shows: Libraries often devote space for local artwork.

- *All grades*—For multiple years, our local library displayed the annual Vermont Homeschoolers' Art Show during the month of April. Early in the school year, I booked a small display case and the hallway "art gallery" to accommodate 2D and 3D artwork. Participating families were given framing guidelines, and each artist was asked to provide a bio picture and an acrostic poem of their name to accompany their artwork. We concluded each show with a closing celebration and artist recognition.

A sampling of art show pieces

After-school Activities: Our library offers after-school programming for children. This is an opportunity for high school students to teach an activity or share an interest with younger students.

- *Older Middle/High School*—Our World Geography and Arts group coordinated a learn-to-sew activity. Students brought pre-cut fabric squares, sewing machines, an iron, and an ironing board. Children learned to sew as they assembled blocks for baby quilts. This was part of a larger service project to make quilts for local refugees.

Left: Community baby quilt projects. Right: A collaborative quilt made by geography students.

Preschool Audiences: Preschoolers are an ideal audience for elementary-age performers. Young students can relate to preschoolers, as preschoolers also look up to their older peers.

Example: *Elementary/Early Middle School*—We adapted a picture book into a play. What began as a casual activity with three other families grew into a library performance for preschoolers.

<u>Cast and Crew:</u> The cast ranged from six to ten years old with an equally wide range of personalities, from shy to gregarious.

<u>Choosing a Picture Book:</u> Children brought book-to-play suggestions. We read them together and chose *The Gruffalo* by Julia Donaldson.

<u>Writing the Play:</u> Roles included the Gruffalo, the narrator, and six unique animals chosen by cast members. Unusual animal choices included a skunk with a spray bottle of lavender water and a piranha who finished each of his lines with chomping sounds. Working with a parent, older students adapted the book to the play, cleverly writing each animal's lines in rhyme.

<u>Play Preparations:</u> Children crafted their own masks and costumes. An extra large box was repurposed as a stage set. The cast and crew planned, drew, and painted.

<u>Performance:</u> This was a child-centered, parent-supported production of utter perfection! Cast members supported each other with lines, entrances, and exits. A parent sat in the front row giving lines and guidance as necessary. One child initially held her mamma's hand while going on and off stage, gaining the confidence to speak her lines. The Gruffalo's box head limited the actor's vision, so fellow actors assisted the Gruffalo on and off set.

The Gruffalo: An Original Adaptation was performed during a mid-morning preschool group. The audience was mesmerized!

<u>Reflection and Learning:</u>

- Takeaway message for me: "My role is safety and support."
- Takeaway message for children: "I can do it! It is safe to be me. I am courageous and I grow!"
- Schedule two to three performances. Kids were nervous before their performance and elated afterward. The growth in each child was extraordinary.

The Gruffalo: An Original Adaptation

Summer Theater Events: Libraries offer summer programming for families and children, making them a great venue for performances and special events. Homeschooling happens any time of the year.

- *Middle/High School*—After graduation, Lauren established the Hourglass Youth Theater, where she directed Shakespeare plays. The theater held summer performances at local libraries and a black box theater. April joined the cast; Aidan joined the music ensemble. A homeschool student composed and conducted original music. Two weeks of rehearsals were followed by a week of performances—a whirlwind of joy!

Shakespeare's **A Midsummer Night's Dream** *performed at local libraries and a black box theater. Aidan created the poster; April played Puck.*

B7. Public Sharing: Students as Teachers

Presentations: Opportunities for students to share what they know builds their confidence and courage.

Older Middle/High School—In our year-long study of World Geography and Arts, the five students chose a topic of interest to research and present on for each of the seven geographic regions we studied. Some examples of students' wide-ranging presentation topics included:
- England Through the Eyes of a Travel Show, inspired by Rick Steves
- A Tour of Significant WWI Sites in Belgium and France presented through hand-drawn postcards and "diary entries"
- All About Llamas in the form of a puppet show
- A Lesson in Arabic for Beginners
- A Tour of Petra
- Alternative Modes of Transportation in Cambodia
- A Brief History of Sri Lanka Through English Rule, which was told with puppets, tea, coffee, and Kandy (candy)

Presentations were initially capped at 15 minutes, building to 30 minutes over the year. By year's end, many students were confidently requesting 45 minutes for their final presentations.

Teaching Peers: Teaching peers in a positive environment becomes an empowering experience of leadership for the student-teacher. It also fosters connection, comradery, and learning for peers.

Older Middle/High School—In World Geography and Arts, everyone was the student-teacher at least once during the year. Some of these experiences included:
- WWII timeline and impacts: The student-teacher shared her grandparents' early experiences in Germany (WWII) and the long-lasting impacts of war.
- Russian fairy tales and an associated Mystery Feast.
- A Day of the Dead celebration: Families and friends brought in commemorative items for a centerpiece, enjoyed a class-prepared Mexican meal, and shared memories.

Aidan's teaching activity: A Day of the Dead celebration

Appendix C: April's Fifth Grade Minimum Course of Study (MCOS)

1. Reading and Writing: Communication, adapted from a fifth-grade workbook:

   a. Grammar: Review parts of speech, verbs and tenses, and comparative adverbs and adjectives; identify and correct common grammatical errors such as run-on sentences; learn common abbreviations; use commas, apostrophes, and quotation marks.

   b. Vocabulary/spelling: Synonyms, antonyms, homonyms, homographs, homophones, long vowels, uncommon spelling patterns, prefixes, and suffixes.

   c. Reading: Read chapter books together and independently. Find information in resource books using the table of contents, section headings, and index.

   d. Writing: Creative writing, science report, book report, and letter writing.

2. Mathematics: Table of contents from purchased curriculum. Incorporate real-world connections. Examples include cooking, measurements, money, wood projects, and sewing projects.

3. History, Citizenship, and Government: The Great Depression and Dust Bowl. United States mapping: The Great Plains including major rivers, states, and capitals. Vermont study: town historical society resources on the Great Depression era in Vermont.

4. Literature: Autobiographical fiction, *Little House on the Prairie* by Laura Ingalls; historical fiction, *Moon Over Manifest* by Clare Vanderpool; resources on the Great Depression and Dust Bowl; and resources about Native American life on the Great Plains prior to European settlement. Original sources such as children's letters to Eleanor Roosevelt (online archive) and correspondence with grandparents.

5. Science: Explore the scientific method and devise an experiment. Write a science report. Ecosystems: flora, fauna, Earth, and inter-connections.

6. Movement and Health: Ballet, hiking, and outdoor games such as tag, trampoline, x-country skiing; skin care including anatomy, sunburns, vitamin D and the sun, and hydration.

7. Creative Arts: Piano, attend Vermont Youth Orchestra concerts, theater productions, contra-dances, printmaking, puppet making, and art deco.

Appendix D: Beehive Study Example
1930s Great Depression and Dust Bowl

This Beehive Study included Aidan, seventh grade, and April, fifth grade. They explored the topics together. Their final projects were individualized (see Purposes above).

Topic 1: The Great Plains Ecosystem and the Causes of the Dust Bowl

<u>Purpose (Imagination)</u>: Aidan loves science! I mailed the following letter to her.

January 5, 1934

Miss Aidan Palmer, Lead Scientist
United States Department of Agriculture (USDA)

Dear Miss Palmer,

When I took office last year, in addition to a financial crisis, this great nation was facing a complex weather and farming crisis in the Great Plains. This crisis continues. I am committed to environmental changes that address this tragic natural disaster and restore our farmland's fertility. This is a priority.

Currently, there is an over-population of jackrabbits devastating crops of wheat that survived the drought and dust. Dust storms are a near daily occurrence during parts of the year, farmers are going bankrupt as crops fail, and poor nutrition and lung sickness are rampant.

As my lead USDA scientist, I am instructing you to investigate the causes of this disaster and make recommendations. Send me a report on your findings by March 15. Include:

- The Great Plains ecosystem at the turn of the century (1900) and now (1934).
- Changes in farming practices and land use since 1900.
- Natural and manmade factors contributing to this catastrophe.
- Recommendations for healing and restoring the resilient ecosystem.

I value your input and look forward to your report.

Sincerely,

Franklin D. Roosevelt
President of the United States of America

Cycles of Learning:

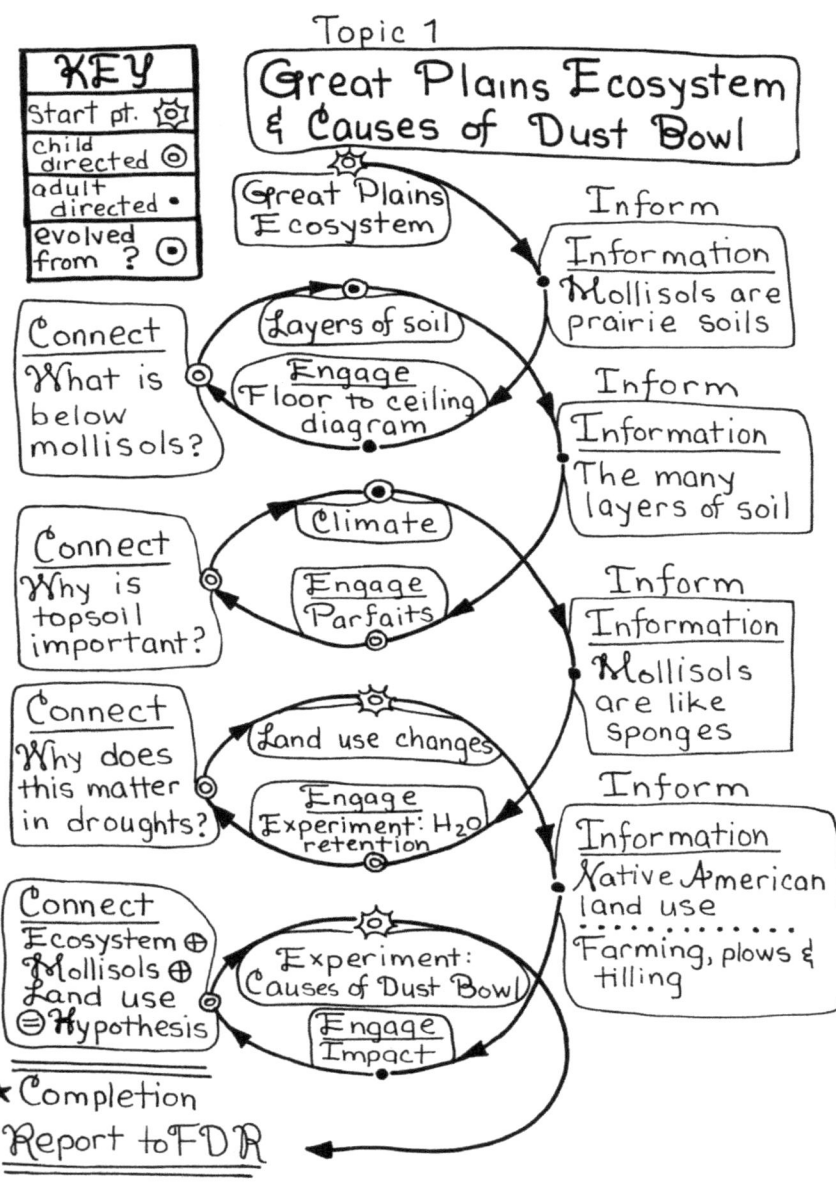

KEY
Start pt. ☼
child directed ◎
adult directed •
evolved from ? ◉

Topic 1
Great Plains Ecosystem & Causes of Dust Bowl

Great Plains Ecosystem

Connect
What is below mollisols?

Layers of soil
Engage
Floor to ceiling diagram

Connect
Why is topsoil important?

Climate
Engage
Parfaits

Connect
Why does this matter in droughts?

Land use changes
Engage
Experiment: H₂O retention

Connect
Ecosystem ⊕ Mollisols ⊕ Land use ⊖ Hypothesis

Experiment: Causes of Dust Bowl
Engage
Impact

Inform
Information
Mollisols are prairie soils

Inform
Information
The many layers of soil

Inform
Information
Mollisols are like sponges

Inform
Information
Native American land use
············
Farming, plows & tilling

★ Completion
Report to FDR

Basic flow of Topic 1 (details follow)

The Great Plains Ecosystem Information: Mollisols are prairie soils.

- Diagram: We created a diagram using floor-to-ceiling paper then drew a horizon line halfway down the paper to delineate above and below ground.

- Soil: Mollisols are dark, nutrient-rich, organic, fertile types of topsoil that can be up to three feet thick. They are common across the Great Plains. We drew a line three feet below the diagram's horizon line. Using craft supplies, the girls filled the three-foot space with representations of rich mollisols, fungi, and other life within the soil.

- Flora and fauna: We learned about flora and fauna using resource books, and we added these to the diagram. Prairie grasses, plants, and animals piqued the girls' interests.

Student question: What is underneath mollisols? Information: Soil layers

- We assembled soil layer parfaits in clear plastic cups, choosing natural representations from our backyard for each soil layer.

- The girls extended this activity, creating edible soil layer parfaits topped with a thick layer of homemade cookie-crumble mollisols.

Student question: Why does this matter? Information: Mollisols are like sponges.

- Impromptu experiment: To understand the value of mollisols in a dry climate, we cut two identical-sized materials. Cotton flannel represented the average topsoil depth. Dry kitchen sponge represented the mollisols depth. We filled two bowls with equal amounts of water and added a dry material to each. Once saturated, we removed the materials and measured the remaining water. The girls recorded the results and drew conclusions.

Land Use Changes   Information: Native American and homesteader land use

- We used resource books and video documentaries to provide information.

- The girls' imagination gave the information meaning. For example: People and animals easily walk around obstacles. Can plows and tractors maneuver around obstacles? How might people change the landscape to make it easier to farm? What do you think happens to the living soil if sod is plowed or tilled? What about plants and animals? Additional questions to research and consider flowed as we delved deeper into the subject.

Experiment—Causes of the Dust Bowl   Information: Scientific process

- The girls hypothesized how changes in land use contributed to the Dust Bowl. Together we devised an experiment to test their hypothesis. We grew two bins of winter rye. Once well established, the experiment started. To simulate drought conditions, we did not water either bin for the duration. We "tilled" one tray with a fork each day, leaving the other tray untouched. Both bins then received three minutes of "prairie wind" using a hair dryer. The girls observed and measured soil loss from each tray and recorded their findings daily. After two weeks, we finished the experiment, compared results, and drew conclusions.

Completion and Reflection:

Aidan: Report and letter to FDR
April: Science experiment worksheet

- Teacher reflection: Immersion is motivating. Aidan's investment empowered her self-directed learning.

- Student reflection: This was Aidan's favorite Beehive Study. She enjoyed being an important scientist and an environmental detective.

Topic 2: Life in the 1930s

<u>Purpose (Imagination)</u>: April enjoyed make-believe and cultural exploration. She was tasked with being a 1930s-era child and writing a letter to Eleanor Roosevelt from a Hooverville, as many children at that time did.

<u>Cycles of Learning</u>:

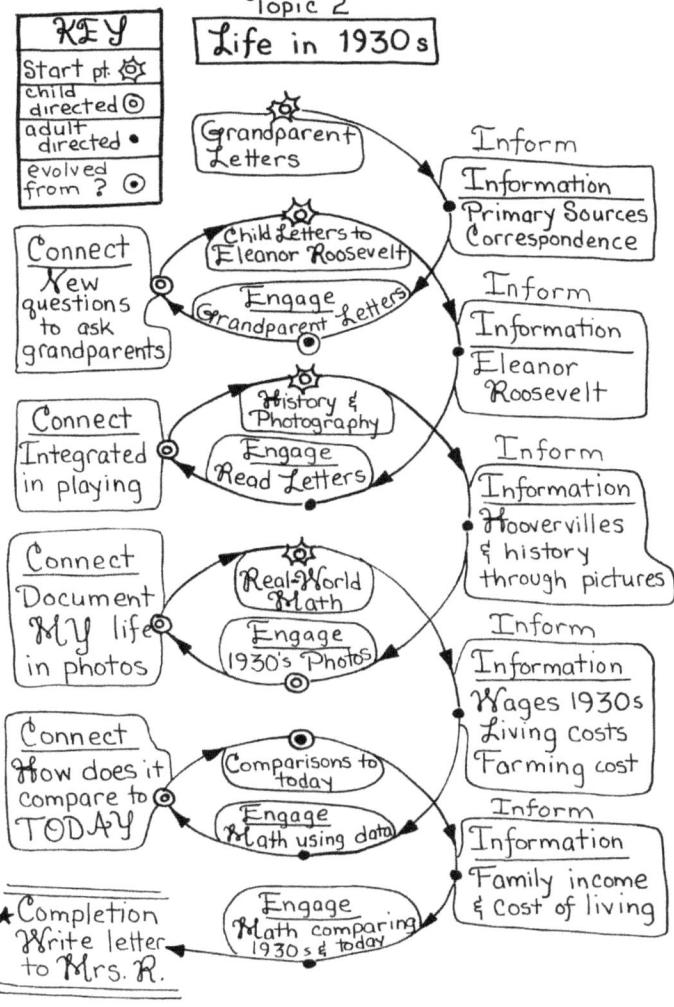

Note: There are online archives of children's letters to Mrs. Roosevelt.

Correspondence with Grandparents   Information: Primary sources

My mother was born in 1928 in the hollers of West Virginia. Below is a portion of her letters about the Great Depression from a child's perspective:

I was young enough to be really scared when so many banks "went under". I remember well when I had to go into our bank with my parents one day and I was crying I was so scared "our" bank "would go under" while we were in there and we would be trapped underground. Later when I was calmer and told them why I was so scared they explained that the building remained where it was but the money was taken away and no longer in the bank. I had money in the bank — put there when I was a baby by my Aunt Xenia for my education: college. Yes, I lost all of that but our bank made good and paid back every dollar eventually to each person who had money in our bank. Maybe not every bank did that.

My father was born in 1920 and grew up on a farm in eastern Kansas during the Dust Bowl. Here is an excerpt from his letters:

Life went on as my nine year mind held that it should with good crops on the farm; rains falling in season; prosperity and a sense of well being generally. Then in 1929 the rains did not fall on schedule, howling winds stirred the arid soil into sky – darkening clouds.

Housewives fought a losing battle with dust accumulating on the window sills and every piece of furniture as well as the floors! Farmers shoveled out dust buried tractors and other machinery. Anyone out doors needed to wear a bandana over mouth and nose. Respiratory diseases increased noticeably.

The previous <u>Cycles of Learning</u> diagram adequately represents the remainder of Topic 2.

<u>Completion and Reflection</u>:

April: Letter to Mrs. Roosevelt
Aidan: Edited report to FDR

- Teacher reflection: Balance topics of less intrinsic interest and high interest. By integrating both, teachers foster students' broader learning. For example, I intermixed challenging real-world math problems with engaging period photographs and children's letters, making math manageable. Unexpectedly, intermixing real-world math also fostered greater insight into photographs and letters. This illustrates the perfect synergy of meeting students' needs!

- Student reflection: Looking at 1930s photography was engrossing, relatable, and imaginative. April enjoyed being a photography detective. Many aspects of this study entered April's free time.

Topic 3: Arts in the Great Depression Era

<u>Purpose (Imagination)</u>: Homeschooler's "Live Action" 1930s day

<u>Cycles of Learning</u>: Planned activities were interwoven with outdoor games.

Soup Kitchen Lunch

- Students brought local vegetables that were cut and ready to be made into soup. Together, they created a soup spice mix, made bread, and churned butter from heavy cream.

"Oregon Trail" by Woodie Guthrie

- The "Oregon Trail" song by Woodie Guthrie chronicles an Oklahoma farmer's plan to take his family to Oregon. It highlights farm life in the Midwest during the Dust Bowl and the farmer's hopes for a better future.

Traditional Music Comes to Life with a Crankie

- A Crankie, or a "moving panorama," is a free-standing frame resembling an open TV screen, with large dowels vertically oriented on either side. I created and tested the Crankie frame before our event. The Crankie gets its name from "cranking" a scrolled picture story across the screen. The students illustrated "Oregon Trail." They taped the pictures together then wound them onto the dowels.
- Low-tech designs can be found online. Our frame was made using sturdy cardboard.

<u>Completion and Reflection</u>:

"Oregon Trail" was performed for parents, accompanied by the moving panorama Crankie.

- Teacher reflection: Students illustrated the entire song, which was a challenge of endurance. In hindsight, illustrating one stanza and the chorus would have worked best, providing more time for outdoor play. Less is often more. This Beehive Study was pivotal in my teaching journey.

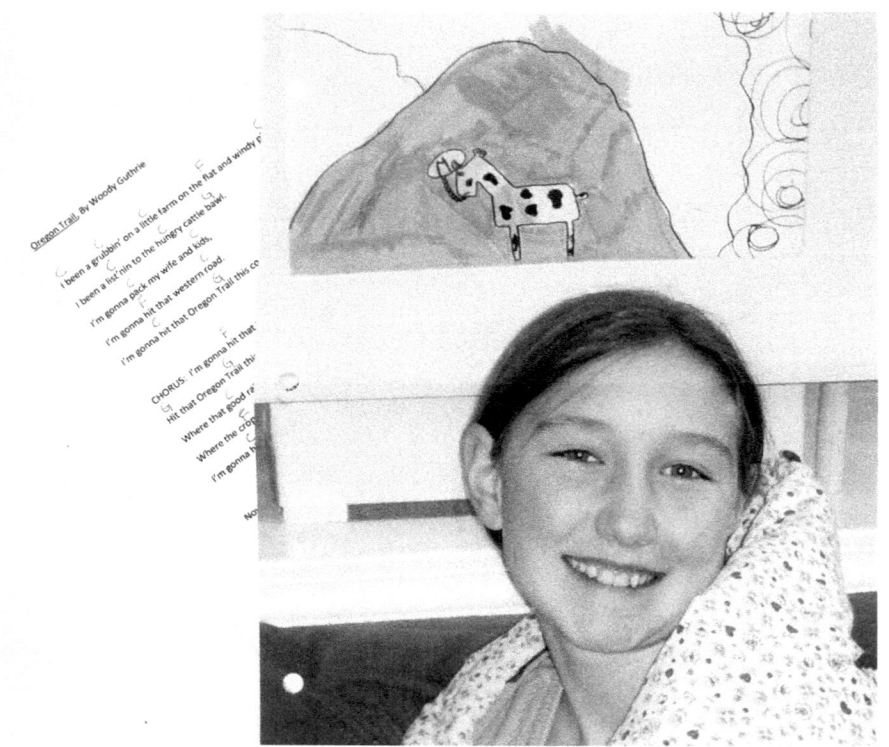

April with her "Oregon Trail" Crankie picture

Appendix E: April's Official Transcript

I have made the following changes to April's official transcript for the purposes of this book:

Bolded courses are followed by course descriptions in Appendix F. Typically no classes are bolded on a transcript.

*** Indicates Beehive Studies. These courses are highlighted here to illustrate how educational *approach* is conveyed in recordkeeping. Typically, the *approach* to education is not highlighted.

A general note about determining credits: 120–180 hours equals 1.0 credit. This equals 4–5 hours a week for most of the school year.

See **Appendix H: Recommended Resources, High School Recordkeeping** for details on crafting transcripts.

Official Homeschool Transcript

Student: April Palmer

School Name: **Joy in Learning**

Graduation: June 18, 2022

Contact Person: Esther Palmer, Homeschool Administrator

Date of Birth: ---

Address: ---

Phone: ---

Level	Course	Class Title	Credit	Grade
9th Grade	Math	Algebra II	1.0	A+ 4.0
	Science	Environmental Science and Earth Stewardship	0.5	A+ 4.0
	Science	Anatomy and Physiology in Motion: Understanding the Human Body for Empowerment and Lifelong Health	0.5	A+ 4.0
	English	*****Young Perspectives: Literature**	**1.0**	**A+ 4.0**
	English	*****Young Perspectives: Writing—Creative and Technical Writing for Self-Expression**	**0.5**	**A+ 4.0**
	Social Studies	*****Historical Panorama of Cultures Through Time**	**1.0**	**A 4.0**
	Fine Arts	Costume Design	0.5	A+ 4.0
	Practical Arts	*****Fabric Arts I: Elements of Design, Technique, and Application**	**0.5**	**A+ 4.0**
	Theatre Arts	*Acting I	0.5	CVU (A)
	Theatre Arts	Community Acting	0.5	Pass
	PE/Health	Integrative Health and Life Sports I	1.0	A 4.0
	Music	*Chorus	0.5	CVU (A)

Level	Course	Class Title	Credit	Grade
10th Grade	Math	Geometry	1.0	A+ 4.0
	Science	Foundational Chemistry and Real-world Applications	1.0	A+ 4.0
	English	Expository Writing: Exploratory and Persuasive Essays (Brave Writer)	0.25	A+ 4.0
	English	Expository Writing: Rhetorical Critique and Analysis (Brave Writer)	0.25	A+ 4.0
	English	Literary Analysis: *Animal Farm* (Brave Writer)	0.25	A+ 4.0
	English	Movie Discussion Club: Sci-fi Mania (Brave Writer)	0.25	Pass 4.0
	Social Studies	Code Women: Making and Breaking Codes	0.5	A+ 4.0
	Social Studies	Colonial to Constitutional USA: Foundational Equality and Democracy	0.5	A+ 4.0
	Theatre Arts	*Acting II	0.5	CVU (A)
	Fine Arts	*Intro to Art	0.5	CVU (A)
	PE/Health	Integrative Health and Life Sports II	1.0	A 4.0
	Practical Arts	Fabric Arts II: Hand Quilting, Dress Design: Pattern Alteration and Construction	0.5	A+ 4.0

Level	Course	Class Title	Credit	Grade
11th Grade	Math	Pre-calculus	1.0	A+ 4.0
	Science	**Physics for the Real World: Classical Beginnings, Big Bangs, and the Infinitesimal**	**1.0**	**A+ 4.0**
	English	MLA Research Essay (Brave Writer)	0.25	A 4.0
	English	Advanced Composition (Brave Writer)	0.25	A+ 4.0
	English	Playing with Poetry: Exploration (Brave Writer)	0.25	A+ 4.0
	English	High School Writing: Current Events (Brave Writer)	0.25	A 4.0
	English	Literary Analysis: Shakespeare's Twelfth Night (Brave Writer)	0.25	A+ 4.0
	Social Studies	***History in Film	1.0	A+ 4.0
	Fine Arts	***History in Film: Artistic Expression and Choice	1.0	A+ 4.0
	Fine Arts	**Landscape in Art (Community College of Vermont)	1.0	CCV (A)
	Fine Arts	Kiri: Intricate Japanese Paper Cutting	0.25	A+ 4.0
	Practical Arts	Fabric Arts II: Hand Quilting, Dress Design: Pattern Alteration and Construction	0.5	A+ 4.0
	PE/Health	Integrative Health and Life Sports III	1.0	A 4.0
	Practical Arts	Fabric Arts III: Quilt Design, Applique, and Hand Quilting; Advanced Dressmaking	0.25	A+ 4.0

Level	Course	Class Title	Credit	Grade
12th Grade	Science	**Natural History Illustration (George Mason University)	0.5	GMU (A)
	English	Transcendentalism: Thoreau and Emerson Past and Present	0.25	A+ 4.0
	English	**Experimentation Versus the Known:** *Peer Gynt* **and** *Frankenstein*	**0.25**	**A+ 4.0**
	English	Literary Analysis: Shakespeare's *Hamlet* (Brave Writer)	0.25	A+ 4.0
	Social Studies	Survey of History: Western World, Renaissance Through Modern Times	0.5	A 4.0
	Social Studies	Psychology and Physiology of Fear: Examining a Global Pandemic	0.5	A+ 4.0
	Fine Arts	Paint on Glass Animation: Storytelling Through Art	0.5	A+ 4.0
	Fine Arts	**Survey of Western Art II (Community College of Vermont)	1.0	CCV (A+)
	Fine Arts	Painting in Oils I	0.5	A+ 4.0

* Denotes class taken at Champlain Valley Union High School (transcripts requested)

**Denotes class taken at colleges (transcripts requested)

Grading Scale

A+   97%–100% 4.0
A   93–96% 4.0
A-   90–92% 3.7
B+   87–89% 3.3
B   83–86% 3.0
B-   80–82% 2.7
C+   77–79% 2.3
C   73–76% 2.0
C-   70–72% 1.7
D+   67–69% 1.3
D   64–66% 1.0
D- /F Below 64% 0.0

Appendix F: Course Descriptions

There is an accompanying course description for each class on the transcript. Here, course descriptions are limited to those bolded on the transcript (Appendix E). They highlight:

- A comprehensive Beehive Study translated into multiple courses
- A student-teacher collaborative course
- An independent class

See **Appendix H: Recommended Resources, High School Recordkeeping** for details on creating course descriptions.

<u>From 9th Grade: A Comprehensive Beehive Study</u>

English—Young Perspectives

Literature: Year. April read and discussed 4 books: *Sense and Sensibility* by Jane Austen (Regency Period); *Great Expectations* by Charles Dickens (Industrial Revolution/ Victorian Era); *Little Women* by Louisa May Alcott (Civil War Era); *Testament of Youth* by Vera Brittain (WWI).

Grading: Attendance: 25%
Homework/Reading: 50%
Midterm and Final: 25%
Credit: 1.0

English—Young Perspectives

Writing—Creative and Technical Writing for Self-expression: Semester. Concurrent with Young Perspectives—Literature. Coursework included: journaling, creative writing, poetry, compare/contrast essays, a persuasive essay, and a research paper.

Grading: Class Participation: 25%
Homework: 25%
Essays: 50%
Credit: 0.5

Historical Panorama of Cultures Through Time: Year. This survey course covered seven historical periods: Ancient Rome, the Vikings, the Regency Era, the Industrial Revolution, the Civil War, WWI, and WWII. Focus: general history, technological changes, and social impacts. Each unit culminated in a final project. This class provided historical context for English—Young Perspectives.

Grading: Class Participation: 50%
Final Projects: 50%
Credit: 1.0

Fabric Arts: Elements of Design, Technique, and Application: Semester. In this self-designed course, April explored hand crafts of the 1800s: embroidery techniques, whitework, beading, three-dimensional fabric embellishments, clothing design, and construction.

Grading: Projects Research and Planning: 50%
Finished Projects and Reflection: 50%
Credit 0.5

From 11th Grade: A Teacher-student Collaborative Class

Physics for the Real World: Classical Beginnings, Big Bangs, and the Infinitesimal: Year. First semester included classical physics with lab work. Topics: forces and motion, Newton's Laws of Motion; work and energy, Laws of Thermodynamics; waves; and electricity and magnetism. Second semester included physics of the very large and very small. Topics: Einstein's Theory of Relativity; the Milky Way and the Universe; and the Big Bang Theory and quantum concepts.

Grading: Participation and Labs: 50%
Homework/Projects: 50%
Credit: 1.0

From 12th Grade: An Independent Class

Experimentation Versus the Known: *Peer Gynt* and *Frankenstein*: April planned and facilitated this six-week online class with peers. Weekly participation included: synchronous online discussion and student-posted questions/short essays. Additional readings from: *Rockefeller Medicine Men: Medicine and Capitalism in America* by E. Richard Brown, and ancient passages including the Bible. Class concluded with a thematic essay or character analysis.

Grading: Homework and Discussions: 50%
Class Planning and Essays: 50%
Credit: 0.25

Appendix G: Easy Print Diagrams

Communication
Listening for Understanding

Communication
Content

words
behavior
observable
skills, tests,
results

seen

communication
Meaning

inner world

fatigue
health
emotional state
development
misunderstood/understood
inexperience/experience
learning style
personal pacing

unseen

Where my
child is

Core

Good   Perfect   Loveable

Who my
child is

Active Listening

Seek to understand  communication **Content**

"I am curious about what is going on in<u>side</u>."

Remember
Who I am
Who my child is 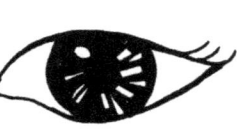 "I see the best in myself and my child."

Discern
Where I am
Where my child is  "I listen for **Meaning**."

Accept
Responsibility "I am the adult and meet my child's needs."

Rules for Life

I am responsible for myself and to myself.
I create my own experiences and feelings.
When I speak, I say more about myself as what I say about the
other person.
At any given time, I am doing the very best that I can do.
I can always be kind and gentle with myself.

—Louise Dietzel, Psychologist-Master

Self-Knowing

Close Your Eyes. Fall in Love. Stay There.

–Rumi

Close Your Eyes	Fall in Love	Stay There
I *create* my inner experiences and feelings.	I am doing my best. I can be kind and gentle with myself.	I accept responsibility. I am the adult.
I *focus* on my best choices. Strong emotions invite immature reactivity. *I stay out of emotions.*	I listen to and follow what I KNOW.	What I say and do is about me. It reflects my *inner* state.
Breathe!	I love and respect myself.	I model maturity for myself. I say what I mean, and I follow through.

Connecting Curriculum Plan and Process

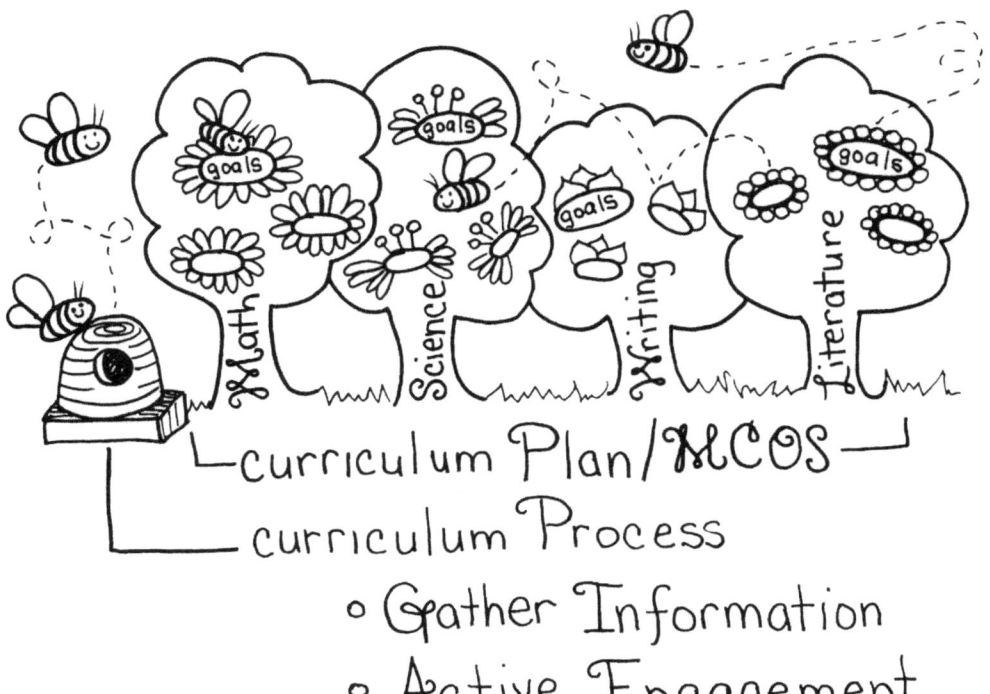

Curriculum Plan/NCOS

Curriculum Process

- Gather Information
- Active Engagement
- Expand Personal Connections & understanding

Appendix H: Recommended Resources

<u>Self-awareness</u>:

De Mello, Anthony. "Your True Power Lies in the Present Moment." [Video] *Wake Up Humanity, YouTube*, https://www.youtube.com/watch?v=k3gCW0h_1HE

Emerson, Ralph Waldo. *Self-Reliance* and *Nature*. 1841, 1836.

<u>Inspirational Teaching Videos</u>:

Damon, Nat. "The Art of Possibility with Benjamin Zander." *Reach Teach Talk Podcast*, May 18, 2022,
https://www.youtube.com/watch?v=nPhXitzy51c

Robinson, Sir Ken. "Do Schools Kill Creativity?" *TED Talk*, January 2007,
https://www.ted.com/talks/sir_ken_robinson_do_schools_kill_creativity

Robinson, Sir Ken. "How to Escape Education's Death Valley; Educating the Heart and Mind." *TED Talk*, April 2013,
https://www.ted.com/talks/sir_ken_robinson_how_to_escape_education_s_death_valley

Zander, Benjamin. "How to Give an A." *Teacher's TV, YouTube*, February 2012,
https://www.youtube.com/watch?v=qTKEBygQic0

Parenting/Adult-child Relationships:

Dietzel, Louise. *Parenting with Respect and Peacefulness*. Starburst Publishers, 1995.

Martell, Beth. *Connected: Defining the Adult-Child Relationship and the Needs We Fulfill Within It*. Self-published, 2024.

Siegel, Daniel and Bryson, Tina Payne. *The Power of Showing Up*. Ballantine Books, 2021.

Tsabary, Shefali. *The Conscious Parent*. Namaste Publishing, 2014.

Adolescent Development:

Cooper-Kahn, Joyce and Dietzel, Laurie. *Late, Lost and Unprepared: A Parent's Guide to Helping Children with Executive Functioning*. 2nd, Routledge, 2024.

High School Recordkeeping:

Binz, Lee. *Setting the Records Straight: How to Craft Homeschool Transcripts and Course Descriptions for College Admissions and Scholarships*. Self-published, 2010.

www.ingramcontent.com/pod-product-compliance
Lightning Source LLC
Chambersburg PA
CBHW041145120626
46547CB00020B/3114